THE GOD WHO KNEELS

The God Who Kneels

A FORTY-DAY MEDITATION ON JOHN 13

✦ ✦ ✦ ✦

Douglas D. Webster

CASCADE *Books* • Eugene, Oregon

THE GOD WHO KNEELS
A Forty-Day Meditation on John 13

Copyright © 2015 Douglas D. Webster. All rights reserved. Except for brief quotations in critical publications or reviews, no part of this book may be reproduced in any manner without prior written permission from the publisher. Write: Permissions, Wipf and Stock Publishers, 199 W. 8th Ave., Suite 3, Eugene, OR 97401.

Cascade Books
An Imprint of Wipf and Stock Publishers
199 W. 8th Ave., Suite 3
Eugene, OR 97401

www.wipfandstock.com

ISBN 13: 978-1-4982-0099-8

Cataloging-in-Publication data:

Douglas D. Webster.

    The God who kneels : a forty-day meditation on John 13 / Douglas D. Webster.

    x + 148 p.; 21.5 cm—Includes bibliographical references.

    ISBN 13: 978-1-4982-0099-8

    1. Bible. N.T. John 13. 2. Foot washing (Rite)—Biblical teaching. I. Title.

BS2615.2 W43 2015

Manufactured in the USA.

Jonathan James Webster

ὁ λόγος σαρξ ἐγένετο

Table of Contents

Preface: Learning to Play John 13 | ix
Day 1: Upper Room Access | 1
Day 2: Jesus is the Host | 5
Day 3: On Bended Knee | 9
Day 4: Prophet-Pastor-Poet | 13
Day 5: Seven Fault Lines | 16
Day 6: The Mind of Christ | 20
Day 7: Deep Theology | 23
Day 8: Inscape | 27
Day 9: Deep Discipleship | 31
Day 10: Table Fellowship | 34
Day 11: Deliberate Action | 37
Day 12: Divine Humility | 41
Day 13: No Reputation | 45
Day 14: Logos Logic | 51
Day 15: Humility and Humiliation | 55
Day 16: Patience | 59
Day 17: Clean Feet and a Pure Heart | 62
Day 18: Holy of Holies | 66

TABLE OF CONTENTS

Day 19: Foot-washing vs. Hand-washing | 70
Day 20: Deliberate Speech | 73
Day 21: I Am | 77
Day 22: Group-Selfishness | 81
Day 23: Luther's Sermon | 84
Day 24: Ego Busting | 87
Day 25: A Betrayer | 90
Day 26: Psalm 41 | 94
Day 27: Facing Betrayal | 98
Day 28: Love Your Enemies | 101
Day 29: Self-Examination | 105
Day 30: Self-Betrayal | 108
Day 31: Treachery | 112
Day 32: Humble Glory | 115
Day 33: A False Literal | 119
Day 34: A New Way to Follow | 122
Day 35: Heroic Spirituality | 125
Day 36: An Ego Challenge | 128
Day 37: The Crowing Rooster | 132
Day 38: Deep Awakening | 136
Day 39: Our Passion Narrative | 140
Day 40: The Third Rejection | 144
Bibliography | 147

Preface

Learning to Play John 13

THE BEAUTY OF THE Gospel narrative, including our focus on John 13, can be likened to a well-made instrument. In the hands of a skilled violinist, a lightweight, fragile piece of finely crafted spruce and maple can fill a concert hall with music. What the violin is to music, the Bible is to meaning. In the hands of a novice, the same violin only squeaks and grates, like fingernails on a chalkboard. No one just picks up a violin and plays beautiful music. It takes years of study and practice. The biblical text and the musical instrument require sensitivity and skill to draw out their true dynamic. I'm not suggesting that we need to be "Bible experts," but we have to "play" John 13 as John meant it to be played. The depth of John 13 is drawn from the truth revealed, and not from ourselves.

Like a violin, the verses of John 13 may appear to be simple and lightweight, but when played with skill, the narrative resonates with truths so profound and moving that we are filled with awe. The biblical text in the hands of a sensitive and skilled interpreter reveals the dynamic meaning that the Spirit-led author intended. Faithful readers and good preachers draw out the meaning of the text the way a great violinist plays music. We want the full range of meaning to be played out not only in our hearing, but in our living. The words and actions of Jesus in the upper room are essential for spiritual formation and ethical impact. Less than twenty-four hours before the crucifixion Jesus gave his disciples a full description of the truth of the atonement and the way of discipleship.

To be attentive to the upper room experience we need a close reading of the text—a *lectio divina* (divine reading). Online surfing and scanning is changing the way we think and affects our meditation on the Word. Our habit of processing data at a rapid clip tends to whisk us past the truth that is meant to fill our minds and hearts and stop us in our tracks. John's narrative art plays to our praying imagination and invites us to become like one of the original disciples. That is to say, that the message intended for them is intended for today's disciple. The same Holy Spirit who reminded the disciples of everything Jesus said continues to remind us (John 14:26). We join the twelve in the upper room. The text is the Spirit's gift to the church. John's vocabulary is simple, his language straightforward, but the impact of the upper room's words and events is incalculable.

These meditations are not spiritual Pop-Tarts with a thin layer of fruity goodness. Comedian Brian Regan has a hilarious take on people who microwave their Pop-Tarts for three seconds because they don't have time in the morning to toast them. Regan warns, "If you are waking and hauling in three seconds, you're booking yourself too tight." The longest meditation here takes about ten minutes to read. If you prayerfully read through the verses in John 13, it will take you a little longer. These theological devotionals are not spiritual sound bites. They require thought and prayer. I don't have a particular reader or "target audience" in mind. I'm writing it up as I see it.

I don't have a communication strategy. That frees me up to say what occurs to me to say, what I'm led to say in the light of the biblical text. I hope that works for you.

DAY 1

Upper Room Access

"Even after Jesus had performed so many signs in their presence, they still would not believe in him. This was to fulfill the word of Isaiah the prophet . . .
 'He has blinded their eyes and hardened their hearts, so that they can neither see with their eyes, nor understand with their hearts, nor turn—and I would heal them.'
 Isaiah said this because he saw Jesus' glory and spoke about him.
 Yet at the same time many even among the leaders believed in him. But because of the Pharisees they would not openly acknowledge their faith for fear they would be put out of the synagogue; for they loved human glory more than the glory of God. Then Jesus cried out, 'Those who believe in me do not believe in me only, but in the one who sent me. When they look at me, they see the one who sent me. I have come into the world as a light, so that no one who believes in me should stay in darkness.'" JOHN 12:37–38, 40–46

We begin outside the upper room. On Wednesday of Holy Week, Jesus and his disciples are with a mixed crowd of *unbelievers*. Unbelief is evident in two distinct ways. The first group's unbelief is obvious because it remains adamant in its refusal to believe in Jesus. Drawing on the Prophet Isaiah, John writes, "He has blinded their eyes and hardened their hearts, so they can neither see with their eyes, nor understand with their hearts, nor turn—and I would heal them" (John 12:40; Isa 6:10). The roots of unbelief go deeper than any claim to freedom of choice. Ultimately, there is no such being as the *sovereign* self. We are not free atoms careening around our own little universes. We are all dependent beings reacting to an array of life-altering forces that we only slightly understand. The unbeliever may characterize his or her state as acute rational awareness or courageous existential honesty, but John characterizes unbelievers as spiritually disabled. They are blind and dumb. There is a negative synergy here between their persistent denial and God's permissive will. Denial has its roots in spiritual blindness. Unbelief is unnatural.

The members of the second group, the *believing unbelievers*, want to believe, but they cannot bring themselves to acknowledge publicly that Jesus is the Christ. John describes this as a clash of glories: human glory versus the glory of God. The crux of the matter is that they are more worried about what people think than what God thinks. Ironically, the pursuit of human glory here is totally religious. If they "openly acknowledge their faith" they will be thrown out of the synagogue. The perversity of this type of unbelief may be worse than outright angry rejection. Religion keeps people from Jesus. A private faith in Jesus is like no faith at all.

There are two groups *outside* the upper room. One group pretty much despises Jesus and the other group is drawn to Jesus, but both groups are on the outside. Unbelief comes in two forms: public denial and private faith. Sadly, the pursuit of human glory, even when it is framed religiously, keeps well-meaning and sincere people from experiencing upper room discipleship.

John's sharp distinction between human glory and God's glory may be jarring. We'd prefer a diplomatic middle way that comforts the undecided and timid, but John is having none of it. My sense is that we should read his description of "outsiders" with our own ears, and not judge how others might react to this verdict: "John is preaching to me." The message is clear: private faith without public confession is really no faith at all. The joyful truth of the gospel is sobering.

Jesus gives the one and only ground for resolving unbelief and he gives it with a shout! To paraphrase, he says, "Look at me and you'll see not only me but the one who sent me." Jesus has said and done everything to substantiate this claim. All that is left for him to do is to declare it. Insider access to the upper room begins and ends with Jesus only. In his light we come to the end of our darkness; the end of our secular cynicism, the end of our religious pride. Change of heart comes from seeing Jesus and ourselves in his true light.

In Daniel Defoe's novel *Robinson Crusoe*, the plot pivots on the gift of repentance. In the providence of God, Crusoe was marooned on a South Pacific island. His solitary life eventually led to deep self-examination. Suffering opened his heart and mind to God. It has a way of doing that. Stripped of everything worldly, he saw himself as he really was, "without desire of good or conscience of evil." He began to lament his "stupidity of soul" and his ingratitude to God. Illness led him to pray for the first time in years, "Lord be my help, for I am in great distress." He began to ask, "Why has God done this to me? What have I done to deserve this?" His conscience checked him, "Wretch! Ask what you have done! Look back upon a dreadful misspent life and ask what you have done. Ask, why you have not been destroyed long before this!"[1]

Like the prodigal son, who ran off to the far country, Crusoe became deeply convinced and convicted of his wickedness. In his anguish, he read this in the Bible: "God exalted him to his own right hand as Prince and Savior that he might give repentance and forgiveness of sins to Israel" (Acts 5:31). His reaction was immediate: "I threw down the book, and with all my heart as well as my

---

1. Defoe, *Robinson Crusoe*, 97, 100, 102.

hands lifted up to Heaven, in a kind of ecstasy of joy, I cried out aloud, 'Jesus, Son of David, Jesus, exalted Prince and Savior, give me repentance!'"[2]

Deliverance from his sin and peace with God meant more to him than being rescued. His redemption was "a much greater blessing than deliverance from affliction. . . . I began to conclude in my mind that it was possible for me to be happier in this forsaken, solitary condition than it was probable I should ever have been in any other particular state in the world; and with this thought I was going to give thanks to God for bringing me to this place."[3]

The story of Robinson Crusoe captures the beauty of upper room access. In a state of utter desolation and abandonment, but without any change in location or circumstances, Crusoe becomes a disciple with upper room access. His soul, no longer marooned and doomed to reside in itself, is at home with God. Jesus is the host. He is seated at the table along with Jesus and the disciples.

Unbelievers, whether resentful or respectful of Jesus, remain on the outside. But upper room access is no secret. The gift of repentance is only a prayer away. God's gracious, nonjudgmental invitation is offered to all. In the clash of glories, God's glory prevails.

Upper Room Reflection

Has either public denial or private faith been a struggle for you?

Does the form of unbelief make it easier or harder to gain upper room access?

How would you describe the "outsider" experience?

Have you ever prayed for the gift of repentance?

---

2. Ibid., 106.
3. Ibid., 106, 126.

DAY 2

Jesus is the Host

"It was just before the Passover." JOHN 13:1

THE CHURCH HAS ALWAYS found Thursday night of Holy Week significant. The name, Maundy Thursday, is derived from the Latin *mandatum*, meaning "commandment." The English words "mandate" and "mandatory" are derived from this Latin origin. The evening was named after Jesus' proclamation: "A new command I give you: Love one another" (John 13:34). What transpired that night between Jesus and his disciples in the upper room continues to guide the church, shape its leadership, and inspire its mission. Maundy Thursday is on the church calendar for a reason. It belongs right there with Good Friday and Easter Sunday. In the upper room, Jesus lays out the meaning of the atonement and true character of discipleship.

ON THURSDAY NIGHT, JESUS gave his followers two simple object lessons during the evening meal. He washed their feet and he broke bread. These two enduring acts go a long way in defining the mission of God and the body of Christ. They merge real hospitality and deep sacrament. The towel, the basin, and the bread and the cup signify the essence of Jesus' kingdom strategy. The Apostle John focuses our attention on the humility of Christ. We read that Jesus "got up from the meal, took off his outer clothing, and wrapped a towel around his waist. After that, he poured water into a basin and began to wash his disciples' feet, drying them with the towel that was wrapped around him" (John 13:4–5).

The familiarity of the scene is like an old picture on the wall hiding in plain view. Too many sermons on this text dull our senses. We've heard the punch line so many times before: "Humble service." Our cynical selves think that Jesus got an awful lot of mileage out of fifteen minutes of ordinary servitude. When the famous do something humble, everyone praises them, but our routine acts of humility and kindness go unnoticed, much less praised. It is with thoughts like this that some of us enter the upper room.

The preparation that has gone into Christ's family meal is almost unfathomable. Nothing less than the grand sweep of salvation history stands behind this meal. At the Last Supper, Jesus is host to three meals in one.

First, this meal is the ultimate family meal. Its meaning is rooted in the Passover and celebrates the exodus, that pivotal redemptive turn in salvation history. Moses and the people of God were given specific instructions: "Each man is to take a lamb for his family, one for each household. If any household is too small for a whole lamb, they must share one with their nearest neighbor, having taken into account the number of people there" (Exod 12:3–4).

Second, this meal is the ultimate sacrificial meal. Jesus celebrated the Last Supper with his disciples on the night that he was betrayed. He also looked ahead to all future believers who would participate in this meal. "For whenever you eat this bread and drink this cup, you proclaim the Lord's death until he comes" (1 Cor 11:26).

Finally, the Last Supper is a farewell meal. "I have eagerly desired to eat this Passover with you before I suffer. For I tell you,

I will not eat it again until it finds fulfillment in the kingdom of God" (Luke 22:15). This ultimate sacrificial family meal is eaten in anticipation of the glorious reunion of the marriage supper of the Lamb. "Blessed are those who are invited to the wedding supper of the Lamb!" (Rev 19:9). This eucharistic family meal has a past, present, and future in salvation history.

At the Last Supper Jesus looks after everything. He gives directions to Peter and John to prepare for the Passover in a large room that he has arranged to be used. He washes the disciples' feet, serves the meal, sets the tone, carries the conversation, and concludes the meal with a blessing. Jesus is still doing what only he can do—"You prepare a table before me in the presence of my enemies" (Ps 23:5). What the psalmist imagined figuratively, Jesus performed literally; Jesus gives us his body and blood. From start to finish Jesus looks after the meal. The setting, the preparations, the conversation, are all under his supervision. He is the host who arranges everything. He is the servant who washes the disciples' feet. He is both high priest and Passover lamb. He is the bread and the cup. The Last Supper is the family meal of all family meals and Jesus is the true host.

The Gospel writers make sure that we feel the suspense and stress that existed outside and inside the upper room. The night was filled with anxiety and fear. The religious leaders were looking "for some way to get rid of Jesus" and the disciples were arguing among themselves "as to which of them was considered to be the greatest" (Luke 22:24). There was outside opposition from the religious authorities, insider betrayal, negative group dynamics, and a sorry state of ugly one-upmanship. This was a tension-filled family meal.

John 13 is the apostle's invitation to attend the Last Supper. He opens the door to the upper room and invites us in. He writes us into the scene, negative thoughts and all, in order to draw out the significance of what Jesus did—not only for the original band of disciples, but for all who follow him. The twelve were there, but they missed the message the first time around. Along with them we need to revisit the upper room to grasp its real hospitality. Our souls are restless and distracted. Sin raises its ugly head. But John's narrative invites us in, regardless of our restless egos, devious ways, and negative thoughts. We are there in the company of the disciples, only half aware and not knowing what to expect. Jesus is the host and he gives us a seat at the table.

Upper Room Reflection

What makes the meal in the upper room meaningful?

How have you accepted Jesus' hospitality?

What do you think about when you celebrate this family meal?

How does the Lord's table fulfill the promise, "You prepare a table before me in the presence of my enemies"?

DAY 3

On Bended Knee

". . . at the name of Jesus every knee will bow."
PHILIPPIANS 2:10

HEAVEN AND HELL MEET in the upper room and we have been invited to take a seat. The image of Jesus on bended knee washing his disciples' feet calls for deep reflection. John slows the narrative down and fills out the details frame by frame. He makes us aware of the devil's role behind the scenes. The dialogue is crafted poetically to reveal the meaning of Jesus' actions and teaching. This powerful scene is best painted in the Spirit, not as a picture on a canvas, but as a vivid experience that shapes our souls and changes our lives. John describes the events of the upper room in a way that invites our reflection and inspires our praying imagination. We intuitively know that Jesus' act of humility and hospitality is something we must pay close attention to and seek to understand.

The Passion Narrative begins with Jesus fulfilling the most basic etiquette of Near Eastern hospitality. He washes the disciples' feet. This act was normally performed by servants, never by the host. If there were no servants to wash the guests' feet, children did the task. Handwashing is personal, it is done by the individual. But foot-washing is communal, a delegated responsibility, provided by the host and performed by servants.

The scene takes us back to Genesis, when Abraham was visited by the triune God at Moriah, some two thousand years earlier in this very same region, Abraham entertained the living God over lunch. One small connecting detail focuses our attention. Abraham bows low and invites his guests to stay, saying, "Let a little water be brought, and then you may all wash your feet and rest under this tree" (Gen 18:4). In Genesis, the hospitality is remarkable but the foot-washing is menial. The work of the servant is simply assumed. Foot-washing etiquette needs no further description and those who perform it receive no recognition. These two foot-washing scenes—that in Genesis and that in the Gospel of John—are significant. They span centuries of divine providence and fulfilled prophecy. Salvation history has run its course from the Abrahamic promise to Christ's passion; from theophany to incarnation; from washing the feet of God before lunch to God washing the feet of the disciples before the Last Supper. Jesus on bended knee washes the disciples' feet.

We are not told explicitly that Jesus is on his knees, but he could not do what he did standing or sitting or even stooping: he had to be kneeling. He had to get down low, hold dirty feet in one hand and a washcloth in the other. Unlike servants who diverted their eyes from their master when they washed their feet, we imagine Jesus looking each disciple in the eye as he washed their feet and then dried them with a towel. They awkwardly looked down on him as he looked up at them. John's vision of the one like a son of man, in the book of Revelation, describes eyes like blazing fire (Rev 1:14). On Patmos, did John recall that penetrating gaze that he saw when Jesus washed his feet? The next day, as Jesus hung on the cross, they looked up at him, and he looked down on them. God himself on bended knee, sees the soul and handles feet, before breaking bread and pouring wine, and before being lifted up on the cross.

Up until now, Jesus was the one before whom people knelt. The Gospels describe these vivid scenes. The shepherds on bended

DAY 3

knee bow low before the infant bundled in strips of cloth and laid in a manger. The magi fall to their knees in the presence of the king. They pay homage to the Christ child. On bended knee they offer their expensive gifts. Kneeling implies more than respect. There is a sense of subservience or worship associated with falling to our knees. In Greek and Roman culture kneeling was discouraged. It was thought to be unworthy of free men and beneath Roman citizens. Aristotle claimed it was a barbaric form of behavior. I imagine most independently minded Americans agree.

At the beginning of Jesus' public ministry, Peter fell to his knees. He pled with Jesus, "Depart from me for I am a sinful man" (Luke 5:8). It appears that plenty of people fall to their knees before Jesus. The rich young ruler came running up to Jesus and fell to his knees. But giving his wealth to the poor and following Jesus was not what he had in mind. He got up off his knees and walked away sad. The woman who snuck into Simon the Pharisees's home to meet Jesus never got off her knees. During dinner she knelt before Jesus and washed his feet with her tears, wiped them with her hair, kissed them and poured expensive perfume on them. Kneeling before Jesus captures the body language of the soul. His presence invokes repentance and reverence. Most Christians know that getting on their knees in prayer is a good place to be. Jesus continues to bring us to our knees.

Even Pilate's soldiers got down on their knees. Within hours of the upper room experience, Jesus was manhandled, beaten, spit upon, and stripped. The Roman soldiers mockingly robed him in scarlet, crowned him with a thorny crown, and forced him to hold a staff in his hand. Jesus meant nothing to them. He became their occasion for expressing contempt for their hated deployment and venting their thinly concealed rage against a people they despised. They knelt down in feigned reverence, laughingly exclaiming, "Hail, king of the Jews!" (Matt 27:29). Their cruelty played out on bended knee in mocking derision. The soldiers made it all a big joke.

Unwittingly, the soldiers symbolize the fact that sooner or later everyone kneels before Jesus: "that at the name of Jesus every knee should bow, in heaven and on earth and under the earth, and every tongue confess that Jesus Christ is Lord, to the glory of God the Father" (Phil 2:10–11). People knelt before Jesus in humble worship. Mocking soldiers knelt in vulgar sacrilege. The one before whom the whole world will kneel knelt to wash the feet of the disciples. The paradox is absolute.

Upper Room Reflection

In your mind's eye, how do you picture this upper room scene?

Jesus, the host, looked after all the preparations, but what was missing?

How has your experience of Jesus brought you to your knees?

What would it have meant to you to look down on Jesus and into his eyes?

DAY 4

Prophet-Pastor-Poet

"One of them, the disciple whom Jesus loved, was reclining next to him." JOHN 13:23

WE KNOW THE STORY line. In the upper room, Jesus washed the disciples' feet, identified Judas as his betrayer, introduced the new commandment, and warned Peter of his denial. But being able to list what happened doesn't mean we really know the story. We don't really know what this text is about until we can describe ourselves the way John described himself: "the disciple whom Jesus loved." We can translate the text from koine Greek into English and still miss the meaning. Familiarity with this famous biblical scene may interfere with our ability to receive this text. Exposure alone does not equal good exegesis or produce life application. Translating this text into transformative truth calls for prayer and a special kind of attentiveness.

Think of the Spirit-inspired apostle as a poet painting a literary Rembrandt. Every square inch of the canvas deserves out scrutiny. Without a hint of embellishment, John paints with words. He nuances the truth and brings the message home. This rough-hewn Galilean fisherman turned prophet-pastor-poet wove story and dialogue together in a way that invites our deep reflection. The Hellenists looked for beauty in works of art detached from the observer, such as magnificent statues and impressive columns. The Hebrews looked for beauty in the integration of life and meaning, gray hair on an old man, a mother surrounded by her children. Beauty is not observed as an object over against oneself; beauty is beheld in the midst of life. This is the beauty we experience from the inside.

We are on the inside. Upper room access changes the way we see and hear Jesus. We identify with John. We, too, are beloved disciples. John leads us away from the admiring crowd toward authentic discipleship. Like the poet-pastor himself, we qualify as "the disciple whom Jesus loved." John never meant this as a boast but as a blessing. His endearing and self-effacing way of identifying himself offers no hint of one-upmanship. He is loved the way Jesus means to love all his disciples. We should not confuse intensity with exclusivity. When our children were younger, my wife and I used to say to each of them, "I love you best," and they knew exactly what we meant.

Jesus accused the religious leaders of his day of possessing the Scriptures but not hearing the voice of God:

> "You have never heard his voice nor seen his form nor does his word dwell in you, for you do not believe the one he sent. You study the Scriptures diligently because you think that in them you possess eternal life. These are the very Scriptures that testify about me, yet you refuse to come to me to have life." John 5:37–40

Jesus said this to so-called "churchmen" steeped in the Scriptures. These Bible scholars had memorized large portions of Scripture. They loved the books of Moses and held them in the highest esteem. But they still didn't get it. Their small world of religious ritual and tradition was an end in itself. They were indifferent to God's salvation-making, history-defining Living Word. They did not hear the voice of God. Instead of being transformed by the Word of God, they molded the Bible into their image. They never internalized the message for themselves or read the Bible along its prophetic trajectory. Instead of participating in the drama of salvation history, they stood apart from it, detached, disengaged, and ultimately against the Bible. Yet they thought they had it down pat.

Meditation on the biblical text navigates between the twin dangers of overthinking and underthinking. By overthinking, I mean concentrating on some alleged problem of the text or delving into some intriguing linguistic feature of the text while ignoring the real message. I doubt if anyone could ever overmeditate on John 13, but someone could study the passage without ever embracing the humility of Jesus. In biblical scholarship and popular preaching we face these twin dangers. If we're not careful we could be left on the outside. Meditation is our way in. Biblical and theological scholarship serve as our escorts. Prayer unlocks the door. The Holy Spirit opens our minds. Jesus welcomes us. John identifies himself as "the disciple whom Jesus loved." By the grace of God this is our shared identity. Our value and significance comes from being loved by Jesus. The Father's glory fills the room.

Upper Room Reflection

What draws you in or distances you from this biblical text?

How do you identify with John, the beloved disciple?

Why is John 13 more descriptive than prescriptive?

What has to change in our lives in order to say we understand John 13?

DAY 5

Seven Fault Lines

"You do not realize now what I am doing, but later you will understand." JOHN 13:7

THE HANDS-ON GOD OF the Bible is on bended knee, handling dirty feet, and teaching the church how to live in the world, how to love one another. No one in Christ ever graduates from this profile. No one rises above Jesus' Beatitudes. Herein lies the secret to salt and light impact and the true wisdom of seeking Christ's kingdom and his righteousness first. No disciple escapes the Great Commandment or retires from the Great Commission. In Christ, we are all called to salvation, service, sacrifice, and simplicity. We belong to the order of the towel and basin. The whole of John 13 becomes a community distinctive, a mark of the body of Christ more important than any denominational distinctive; not the ritual of foot-washing that some groups practice literally, but the theological and ethical thrust of what Jesus said and did.

We are tracking the descent of the Son of the Most High, who descends lower and lower. The act of foot-washing is Jesus' final parable. On bended knee he explains the atonement through the metaphor of cleansing. He mentors discipleship through example

DAY 5

and exposition. The wisdom of the household of faith cannot rise above the parable, proclamation, and passion of John 13. This chapter has much to teach us about following the Lord Jesus and what it means to be the church.

On day five it is important that we lay out an overview of this seminal scene for Christian discipleship. On the surface it may look deceptively simple, but seven fault lines run below the surface of John 13. Meditation explores these tensions in the text and unearths the passion of the passage. Each one of these tensions will be explored in the days ahead.

The first tension is between an overly familiar reading of the text and the Apostle John's Spirit-inspired meaning of the text. Familiarity allows us to pass over this text without discerning the difference between admiration and discipleship. We may be tempted to read and preach this passage as a moralistic object lesson, but the Holy Spirit intends much more in Jesus' act and interaction. Ironically, the text of choice for motivating church volunteers dulls our sensitivity to the meaning of the text. We need a fresh reading, one that opens up the meaning and intensity of John's narrative.

The second tension is between the doctrine of the atonement and the praxis of discipleship. There is an essential connection between the meaning of Christ's sacrifice on the cross and the Jesus way of sacrificial service. The crucified Lord of all is preaching to us from his knees and he invites us to join him in the sacrificial life of discipleship: "to love one another as I have loved you."

The third tension is between Jesus' Passion Narrative and our life narratives. We are sometimes slow to realize that Christ's Passion Narrative has turned each of our lives into a passion narrative. We are not detached observers watching Jesus' drama. We are seated at the table of broken bread and poured out wine. We are called to follow the crucified Lord.

The fourth tension is between Jesus' deliberate action and our obedience. We like the idea of free grace and no-load discipleship. Jesus didn't wash our feet and go to the cross so that we could realize our potential and feel successful. The intensity of the upper room is not religion as usual.

The fifth tension is between Jesus' humility and our quest for honor. The meaning of the upper room ought to pervade every sanctuary, boardroom, lecture hall, living room, and kitchen. I may preach humility but I am tempted to practice hubris. Where do self-promotion, institutional pride, and expensive public relations fit in the ethos of the upper room? John 13 offers a fresh understanding of spiritual ambition. We ought to ask ourselves, how do we keep up with the God who kneels?

The sixth tension is between Judas's betrayal and Peter's denial. We ignore the personalities seated at the Last Supper at our peril, because we are very much like this company of confused and conflicted individuals. The great Reformer Martin Luther was not as ready to write off Judas as a singular aberration of evil as we may be. He saw the likes of Judas and Peter in the church of his day. The tensions around that table are with us today. We are still coping with betrayal and denial around the Lord's table and in the boardrooms of our churches. We are a mixed bag both within ourselves and within the congregation.

The seventh tension is between divine humility and divine glory. Many of us have been trained to separate the theology of the cross from the theology of glory, but Jesus insists on keeping them together. This is evident in the upper room. We cannot have the cross without the glory of God and we cannot have his glory without the cross. Humility and exaltation belong together. They are inseparable. But this glory has nothing to do with worldly glory and power, nothing to do with success in the eyes of the world. The incarnate God who kneels shows us the glory of the Father's love and approval.

In the days ahead we will explore these tensions in the text. To the degree that we identify with Jesus, his person and his work, we live in these tensions. But it is exactly these tensions that we have largely lost in contemporary Christian communication. We have obscured the polarity between Jesus-like lowliness and worldly success. We have blurred the distinction between human glory and God's glory. We have blended Jesus-centered truth and cultural conformity.

DAY 5

The Danish Christian thinker Søren Kierkegaard called this sorry state Christianity without Christ. The Christianity of his day had taken on a religious life of its own—divorced from the message and method of Jesus. Instead of teaching people how to follow Jesus, preachers inspired congregations to admire Jesus. Kierkegaard accentuated the difference between discipleship and admiration. He called Christians to take up their cross and follow Jesus.

When we ignore the tension in the text, Christian communication becomes repetitive and boring. True meditation draws us into the real tension between the Word of God and the way of the world. We wrestle with sin and salvation, judgment and worship, law and grace. Real reflection confronts us with the fallen human condition and God's redemptive provision. Jesus' message in the upper room is light-years away from the religious info-sermon and the latest self-help drivel. He embodied his final parable. His actions and words corresponded perfectly. Message and method converged in a sermon that exposed the fault lines running between conventional religious thinking and the gospel. If at first you don't understand this, give it time. As you read and reread John 13, Jesus, John, and the Holy Spirit will make sense of it for you, and you'll find surprising life applications. We may not realize the depth of this truth at first, but Jesus promised "later you will understand."

Upper Room Reflection

What does it mean to belong to the order of the towel and basin?

Which of the tensions in the text challenges your understanding of discipleship the most?

How have you experienced the difference between admiring Jesus and following Jesus?

What strategies or excuses do we use to evade the order of the towel and basin?

DAY 6

The Mind of Christ

"Jesus knew that the hour had come for him to leave this world and go to the Father." JOHN 13:1

JESUS ON HIS KNEES is not about a great man condescending to do a menial task in order to inspire his followers to be humble. This moralistic reading of John 13 skims the surface and misses the meaning of the text. What appears simple on the surface—a towel and basin, and the menial work of a servant—was intended by Jesus to reveal the unfathomable mystery of God's great love and sacrifice. Jesus deliberately performs a prophetic act "that will interpret to the disciples that terrible event which they cannot now understand."[1] A moralistic reading of the text may inspire admiration for Jesus but it does so at the expense of theological truth. It is all about Christ's atoning sacrifice and sacrificial discipleship.

---

1. Newbigin, *The Light Has Come*, 167.

DAY 6

A FAITHFUL PASTOR PREACHED on "loving service" from John 13. He did a fine job presenting the necessity of foot-washing for a group of men walking the dusty dirt paths of Palestine in the first century. He emphasized the awkwardness around the table as none of the disciples deemed it their responsibility to take on the role of a servant and wash the disciples' feet. No one was willing to humble themselves even though it was a breach of etiquette to recline at the low table with unwashed feet.

The preacher noted that Jesus' loving service issued out of his fullness. Jesus didn't need to be needed. There was nothing lacking in his life that needed to be fulfilled by giving himself away to others. To illustrate this the pastor said, "It is like the popular high school senior who goes out of her way to reach out to an unpopular girl." But then he added, "I can't say that of a junior high girl, because if a popular junior higher reached out to an unpopular student, she would immediately become unpopular." His unintended aside unwittingly backed into the tension in the text. The illustration of the popular high school student who lowers herself to reach out to others fit his theme. Altruistic kindness has its rewards. Lower yourself to help others and people will think more highly of you. Servant-hearted kindness to those in need is love in action and cultivates self-respect. But the disciples were not buying this take on Jesus' actions. They were embarrassed. The text forces us to go deeper.

What Jesus did in the upper room provoked the disciples' disapproval, not their admiration. When Jesus strips down and begins to wash the disciples feet, he becomes, at least in Judas' mind, like the junior high student who reaches out to the unpopular girl—despised and rejected. A disillusioned Judas, with his hopes dashed, must have been filled with disdain for Jesus. The prophet Isaiah summed it up this way: "Like one from whom people hide their faces he was despised, and we held him in low esteem" (Isa 53:3). Ted Turner, the founder of CNN, famously said, "Christianity is a religion for losers. I don't want anyone to die for me."

John makes us aware of the immediacy of Jesus' death. The movement of this entire scene is deeply theological. Foot-washing serves as an object lesson. It is Jesus' final parable and its significance lies in the cross—Christ's atoning death. The Passion Narrative begins now, hours before Gethsemane and the betrayal. John makes foot-washing and the cross one continuous expression of Jesus' love.

John sets up this scene with a sevenfold emphasis on the meaning of Jesus' death. He clearly intends something more than a story about service. Jesus' foot-washing is a prophetic act symbolizing the redemptive cleansing that only he can provide. The meaning of God's sacrifice and the method of God's mission are proclaimed visually and verbally by the God who kneels. In the upper room Jesus on bended knee illustrates divine cleansing and new commandment love. John's austere narrative does this deftly without belaboring a point. The Apostle John begins with the Passover, God's long-standing redemptive reference point, to frame all that is said and done. With poetic intensity and simplicity, John links the Passover to the soul-cleansing power of the atonement. He causes us to think of Jesus, the Passover Lamb who takes away the sin of the world. Loving service is rooted in the atonement.

Upper Room Reflection

Why does a moralistic take on Jesus' actions fall short?

Can you identify with the disciples' embarrassment over Jesus' actions?

What aspect of the Christian life remains difficult for you to accept?

Can you explain why this is more than a good story about service?

DAY 7

Deep Theology

"Having loved his own who were in the world, he loved them to the end." JOHN 13:1

THE MEANING OF JESUS' death is the focus of John's descriptive details. John framed the scene to underscore the significance of the cross. Yesterday we reflected on John's first redemptive marker, the Passover. The second deep meaning indicator is his reference to the *hour*, God's kairos timing. Jesus is aware "that the hour had come for him to leave this world and go to the Father." Throughout his Gospel, John tracks the expectation of the hour (2:4; 4:21–23; 5:25, 28; 7:6, 30; 8:20; 12:23). This is the hour in which the Son of Man will be glorified and the will of the Father will be accomplished. This is the hour that finally arrived on Thursday night. The Passion Narrative had begun. God's grace-filled timing was set in motion. It was the final countdown to the cross and the resurrection.

The third marker is John's reference to Christ's love, which clearly shows that there is much more here than a morality play or a random act of kindness. This love is the enduring, eternal, redemptive love of Jesus. This love extends from foot-washing to the cross. "Having loved his own who were in the world," recalls an earlier line from John's prologue, "he came unto his own, but his own received him not." Christ's love prevails in spite of rejection. The timing is right for Jesus to show the full extent of his love, not just to his immediate band of disciples, but to all of "his own who were in the world." The limitless nature of this love is captured in the ambiguity of the meaning of telos. The sentence can read, "He loved them to the end," or it can read, "He loved them to the utmost." Either way, we hear echoes of John 3:16, "For God so loved the world that he gave his one and only Son that whosoever believes in him shall not die but have everlasting life." This is the deep, soul-cleansing love of sins forgiven, guilt removed, and righteousness bestowed.

The fourth deep meaning indicator is John's matter-of-fact reference to the devil. Whether moderns are embarrassed or shocked doesn't matter; the reality stands: the devil is influential, persuasive, and determined. The personal presence of supernatural evil manipulating the heart and mind of Judas is acknowledged by John as a fact. The devil's prompting plays on Judas' sin-induced vulnerability. Upper room access is no guarantee of immunity from evil's infection. On bended knee, Jesus is heading to the cross. Everything has been set in motion. The momentum is building and even the forces of evil are unknowingly governed by God's sovereign redemptive will.

John's fifth theological truth offers a behind-the-scenes explanation. He frames the Passion Narrative with the very highest view of Christ. "Jesus knew that the Father had put all things under his power, and that he had come from God and was returning to God; so he got up from the meal . . ." John shapes the reader's upper room understanding with post-resurrection perspective. Sometime during the forty days before the ascension the risen Christ briefed the disciples on what he knew and how he felt leading up to the cross. The abiding presence of the Father and the purpose of his will never left him. John remembers observing this confidence and calmness. Jesus' serenity and certainty in the midst of hostility and confidence was manifest in the upper room. The bond between Father, Son and Holy Spirit brings the highest glory of heaven down to earth. Martin Luther said, "He thought of His glory which he had with the Father from all eternity, and which He would now assume as to His human nature."[1]

The sixth indicator may seem implicit to us, but it was deliberate in the mind of John. When he said that Jesus *laid aside* his outer clothing, he recalled Jesus' description of the good shepherd as the one who "*lays down* his life for the sheep" (10:11; see 10:15, 17, 18). The language of *laying aside* or *laying down* makes a significant connection between the foot-washing and the death of Christ.

The seventh and final indicator is the word "finished"—"When he had *finished* washing their feet, he put on his clothes and returned to his place" (John 13:12). It is the same word Jesus used at the very end, when he cried from the cross, "It is finished" (John 19:30). The word "finished" links foot-washing and crucifixion as one continuous divine action.

All seven elements are woven into the tapestry of this scene, helping the church see what she might otherwise miss. The issue in the foreground is not admiration but atonement. Luther believed that the foot-washing scene focuses on the person of Christ and "the washing from sin by His blood shed upon the cross." Luther continued, "Such washing is no example; for we cleanse neither ourselves nor others from sin. The Son of God, the Lamb of God, who bore the sins of the world, can do it, and He alone."[2]

Jesus turned foot-washing into a preview of the cross. The mundane act of washing feet is transformed into a redemptive analogy. The story is not about a great man condescending to do something nice; it is about God incarnate descending and dying for the sake of our salvation. The moralistic angle doesn't work and best business practices miss the point. This isn't about random acts of kindness. This is about the mercy of God, eternal salvation, and costly discipleship. Jesus has the cross in mind and so should we.

1. Luther, "Sermon for the Thursday Before Easter," 24–25.
2. Ibid., 26.

Upper Room Reflection

Does foot-washing lose its spiritual force if we see it as a metaphor for self-denial?

How does John make the case for a metaphoric meaning of foot-washing?

Which deep meaning indicator had the greatest impact on you?

What are the implications of the Passion Narrative beginning with foot-washing and ending in crucifixion?

DAY 8

Inscape

"You do not realize now what I'm doing..." JOHN 13:7

POET GERARD MANLEY HOPKINS coined the term "inscape" to describe the unique character of an object or subject as it relates to its environment. Landscapes give us the horizon. Inscapes give us the essence. In John 13, John develops a theological *inscape* for the nature and practice of discipleship.

What gives foot-washing a cross-bearing significance? To answer this question, we take John's seven deep meaning indicators and reapply them to Jesus' followers. I believe it is important for us to see them all together. What I have done here is take what was said yesterday about Jesus and apply each theological marker to his followers. Here are the seven again: the Passover, kairos timing, redemptive love, the work of the devil, Jesus' self-identity, his self-emptying, and his finished work. We are meant to transpose all seven indicators into a score to be played out in the life of the believer. We are playing "second fiddle" to the concert master, but what a privilege to play in this symphony!

We begin with the Passover, the event that underscores the meaning of redemption not only for the Savior but for his disciples. By divine design everything in our lives is to be framed by God's redemptive action. Christ's disciples embrace life sacramentally. Nothing lies outside the scope of God's redemption, from menial household duties to evangelism. Because of Christ's death we are continuously dying to self and to the old sin nature. In Christ we are made alive to the positive richness of life as intended and redeemed by God. We no longer live, but Christ lives in us, and the life that we now live we live by faith in the Son of God who gave himself for us (Gal 2:20). Salvation is grandly inclusive of all we are and will be.

The second deep meaning indicator, applied first to Christ and then to us, is time. As Jesus was conscious of his "hour," we become conscious of a new sense of time and timing. Life is not primarily measured in minutes and months but in God's providential will. The old chronology of the past, with its Rolex pride and self-importance, gives way to God's rhythms of grace. Instead of pursing present-moment happiness we learn to abide in Christ moment by moment.

The third marker is love. Jesus showed the world the full extent of his love, and he calls his disciples to do the same. We are not only the recipients of his love but the agents of his love. We love because he first loved us.

The fourth shared factor between the Master and his disciples is the devil. The devil's real presence in the upper room is consistent with his real presence in the world. Our struggle is not against flesh and blood, but "against the powers of this dark world" (Eph 6:12). Like a wounded animal the devil roams around seeking those he may devour (1 Pet 5:8).

The fifth deep meaning indicator, Jesus' divine self-identity, is the basis of the believer's resilient self-confidence. Because Jesus "knew the Father had put all things under his power, and that he had come from God and was returning to God," we know who we are. We can say with the Apostle Paul, "I am what I am" by the grace of God (1 Cor 15:10).

DAY 8

The sixth parallel between Jesus' cruciform identity and the disciple's calling is self-denial. As Jesus laid aside his clothes as a precursor to laying down his life, we deny ourselves and take up our cross daily and follow him. His path to the cross is our path to the cross.

The seventh indicator focuses on the word *finished*, which is used when Jesus is done washing the disciples' feet. It is the same word, the seventh word, Jesus uttered on the cross, when he said, "It is finished." Between these two uses of the word *finished* we have the spectrum of Christlike service. The finished work of Christ reminds us of the unfinished work of our calling. It is precisely because of Christ's gift of salvation by grace that we have a holy vocation. If God were not working in us to will and to act according to his good purpose, our service would be pointless. We cannot add to what Christ accomplished through the cross and the resurrection, but we can participate in his work. The finished work of Christ calls us to action. This is why the Apostle Paul said, "I fill up in my flesh what is still lacking in regard to Christ's afflictions, for the sake of his body, which is the church" (Col 1:24).

These seven parallels between Jesus and his followers lay the foundation for the believer's self-identity and deliberate action. This vivid picture of Jesus on bended knee is a defining moment for all of us who seek to follow Jesus. True spirituality is a grace-filled process that allows Christ's life to take shape in ours by the power of the Holy Spirit. As we meditate on this scene, the inscape of Jesus' action takes shape in us. The interior landscape belongs to Jesus and he calls us to follow his example. Out of his glorious riches may he strengthen us with power through his Spirit in our inner being, so that Christ may dwell in our hearts through faith (Eph 3:16–17).

Upper Room Reflection

What is the significance of applying the seven deep meaning indicators to Christ's disciples, as well as to Christ?

How do these indicators expand our understanding of what it means to *accept Jesus*?

Which marker has the greatest impact for you?

What does it mean for us to say that Christ's path to the cross is our path to the cross?

DAY 9

Deep Discipleship

"Do you understand what I have done for you?"
JOHN 13:12

THE HUMILITY OF JESUS is best interpreted by Jesus himself. We resist the temptation to read into his action motives of our own. Jesus stripped down to wash the disciples' feet but we cannot strip the text of its theological meaning. He removed his outer clothes, but we must not remove the inner meaning of his actions. Well-intentioned interpreters congratulate Jesus for being "the best manager and developer of human resources the world has ever seen." They like what they see on the surface. They leverage the life of Jesus to make a practical point that has nothing to do with the atonement or the practice of discipleship.

Laurie Beth Jones in *Jesus, CEO*, presents Jesus as a leader who knew how to manage people. She claims that when Jesus washed the disciples' feet, he set an example for his staff. He was creating a top-down corporate culture that showed the value of people. He showed them he cared. He believed in his team and he modeled success. When Jones claims Jesus is the epitome of the Omega management style, she conjures up images of Fortune 500 executives who are winsome and savvy.[1] She ignores the meaning of the cross.

Cynics see humility as a clever ploy to get their way, just another strategy for manipulating people, a weapon in the Machiavellian arsenal of domination. In *House of Cards,* Kevin Spacey plays Francis Underwood, a ruthless congressman who stops at nothing to conquer anything and everyone. In a scene back in his home district, Congressman Underwood fakes humble contrition before parents grieving the loss of their daughter. Underwood turns to the camera and says, "What you have to understand about my people is that they are a noble people. Humility is their form of pride. It is their strength. It is their weakness. And if you humble yourself before them they will do anything you ask." Humility, like virtue, can be perverted and used for evil purposes.

More than 500 years ago, Thomas à Kempis wrote *The Imitation of Christ*. His spiritual direction stressed the rigors of discipleship, the deceptiveness of self, and the lusts of the world. He challenged believers to cultivate an in-depth personal awareness of Christ. "Our chief pursuit," wrote Thomas, "is to meditate upon the life of Jesus Christ." Whoever "would fully and feelingly understand the words of Christ must endeavor to conform his whole life to Him."[2]

Thomas goes a long way in distinguishing between spiritual "knock-offs" and the true imitation of Christ. The Jesus model is best observed in humble saints who take up their cross daily even though it is out of sync with the success strategy of the world. Jesus warned, "What people value highly is detestable in God's sight" (Luke 16:15).

Thomas understood the ubiquitous presence and providence of the cross. Foot-washing is the tangible expression of

---

1. Laurie Beth Jones, *Jesus, CEO*. Jones argues that Jesus' approach to leadership is a cross between the Alpha management style, based on the masculine, authoritative use of power, and the Beta management style, based on the feminine, cooperative use of power. The Omega management style "incorporates and enhances them both" (xiii).

2. Thomas, *The Imitation of Christ*, bk. 1, ch. 1, 45.

cross-bearing. And if daily cross-bearing begins with foot-washing it includes everything. Foot-washing is the metaphor for down-to-earth, practical ministry. Jesus on bended knee in the upper room embodies the continuum of the cross, stretching from foot-washing to Calvary. Disciples go with Jesus' interpretation. This is the truth echoed in Thomas's devotional classic:

> The cross, therefore, is always ready; it awaits you everywhere. No matter where you may go, you cannot escape it, for wherever you go you take yourself with you and shall always find yourself. Turn where you will—above, below, without, or within—you will find a cross in everything, and everywhere you must have patience if you would have peace within and merit an eternal crown.[3]

Upper Room Reflection

Have you ever been inclined to think that deep discipleship belongs to others and not to yourself?

Why is it wrong to make Jesus out to be the model businessman?

How can humility be turned into a tool of the devil?

What does Thomas mean when he says that you can find a cross everywhere?

---

3. Ibid., bk. 2, ch. 12, 62.

DAY 10

Table Fellowship

"The evening meal was in progress..." JOHN 13:2

HOSPITALITY IS HOME TURF for the gospel. "The evening meal was in progress..." John's descriptive note reveals the delightful truth that the theology of the cross can be discussed over dinner. Table fellowship fits into the New Testament narrative so unobtrusively that we can almost miss it. A simple meal was the context for much of Jesus' interaction with his disciples. Religion seems to imply that whenever God is the subject, the conversation belongs in a church or some other "sacred space," but that is not the Jesus way. A simple meal is one of the best places to begin to understand and practice true spirituality. God intends for theology to be worked out over a meal together. A prominent Pharisee missed this humanizing truth, but Zacchaeus embraced it.

In his humility, Jesus invites our hospitality. Physical and spiritual nourishment belong together. When we break bread in community we feed on the bread of life. Over dinner we come to understand the will of God. We learn to pray together. We might prefer to keep theology off the table and on the bookshelf, but Jesus didn't give us that option. He turns the dinner table into a pulpit and his pedagogy offers equal measures of relating and reasoning. The upper room is the place to do real theology.

Jesus' teaching style led to conversations along the way and around the table. The disciples felt free to ask questions. There was plenty of give and take in a free-flowing dialogue. The upper room is a great model for family devotions. Without the ambience of authority or sacred symbol, Jesus modeled the open secret of genuine spiritual formation. He appealed to the mind and the heart. He used metaphor and parable, innuendo and hyperbole to reach his disciples. His message resisted take-it-or-leave-it bullet points. Judging from Jesus' example, growing strong disciples is slow and deliberate work. If I expect to follow his example, I need to become more prayerful and creative when it comes to my lunch appointments and dinner conversations. The pedagogy of the table of the Lord does not work on folding chairs facing a video screen, but in real person-to-person conversation.

The evening meal in the upper room occurred with life-threatening hostility brewing on the outside and considerable fear and confusion intruding on the inside. But in the mind of Jesus it was the best place for doing theology. The church is like the disciples in the upper room that night, filled with all the emotions that make disciple-making difficult and challenging. The hospitality of Jesus and the pedagogy of the table set the stage for authentic transformation. Spirituality is often squeezed into a corner of life reserved for pious reflections and church services. But God intended spirituality to be at the center of our ordinary, everyday life together.

> So here's what I want you to do, God helping you: Take your everyday, ordinary life—your sleeping, eating, going-to-work, and walking-around life—and place it before God as an offering (Rom 12:1, *The Message*).

Upper Room Reflection

Why is the kitchen table a good place to have a conversation about the Christian life?

Do you find Jesus' style of hospitality liberating or intimidating?

Is theology best served in three-point sermons or in the give and take of face-to-face conversation?

What is the best way for you to receive spiritual nourishment?

DAY 11

Deliberate Action

"So he got up from the meal..." JOHN 13:4

ON ONE OCCASION WHEN I was preaching on John 13 I got on my knees. The thought of doing this had not occurred to me until I did it. Somehow the body language seemed appropriate in the moment to underscore the scene. For a minute or two I stayed on my knees, describing John's detailed description of Jesus' deliberate action of washing the disciples' feet.

John's upper room commentary is sketched with brevity. His simple narrative is focused like a laser on what counts. There is no extraneous detail. I might like more color commentary, like a description of the disciples' faces and comments as Jesus knelt before them and washed their feet. But most of the disciples in the upper room are not even named and their reactions to Jesus are ignored. John's poetic description focuses on the meaning of Jesus' action. The beloved disciple takes us through frame by frame, freezing the action sequence with a series of still lifes.

Seven verbs describe this simple act of foot-washing. Three verbs define the preparation: Jesus *got up* from the meal, *took off* his outer clothing, and *wrapped* a towel around his waist. Three verbs describe the action: Jesus *poured* water into a basin, *washed* the disciples' feet, and *dried* them with a towel. Six verbs, two groups of three, slow the action down and add to the drama of the moment. The missing verb, making it seven, is the obvious one: Jesus *knelt*. No mention is made specifically of Jesus being on his knees but he could not have done what he did any other way. He got up and laid aside his outer clothing, knelt down, and handled dirty feet. No one expected him to do what he did. Even Jewish servants were not subject to this odorous and humiliating task. These seven verbs, *got up, took off, wrapped, knelt, poured, washed,* and *dried,* emphasize the intentionality of Jesus' action. John's description of Jesus' actions fixes this object lesson of discipleship in our minds—not as a formula, but as a deliberate act.

Humility is neither an unconscious instinct nor a personality trait. I have heard it said that the moment persons think they're humble, they're guilty of pride. But humility is not about being naive or unaware. Humility is an intentional commitment of our will to the will of God. It is a spiritual discipline that requires deliberate action. Humility is a chosen and cultivated quality of character that matures and deepens with the experience of Christ. Humility is resolute self-emptying, the surrender of the will to the commands of God and the needs of others.

Many write humility off as a less-than-cool, churchy sounding topic, that takes advantage of people who suffer from low self-esteem. Critics argue, "In this put-down world of ours, we've had enough of gloomy piety, doormat theology, and self-demeaning put-downs. Give us hope, not humility!" To empathize with people's paranoia about false spirituality and empty piety is one thing, but genuine, honest-to-goodness humility is not the problem; it is the solution. Humility before God is the way out of humiliating guilt tactics and manipulation.

Humility is love in action. The action verbs, highlighted in John's narrative, carry soulful impact. In his epistle, John spells out the practical implications explicitly, "If any one of you has material possessions and sees a brother or sister in need but has no pity on that brother or sister, how can the love of God be in you? Dear children, let us not love with words or tongue but with actions and truth" (1 John 3:17–18).

A friend spent twenty years listening to sermons and attending Sunday morning Bible classes before he began to take Jesus seriously. Although Ray felt he was a sincere believer, he admits in hindsight that following Jesus had virtually no impact on his life and no influence on his business career. For Ray the Bible was a book of idealistic platitudes and pious sayings. It belonged in the church, not the workplace.

A serious car accident and some deep soul-searching proved to be Ray's wake-up call. He began asking himself what it meant to follow Jesus *everywhere*. By God's grace he began to read and study the Bible with a new set of eyes. He internalized the Word of God and began to act on his newfound convictions. Ray prayed through the way he did business. He set new priorities and embraced new values. His family became more important to him than his career. Some changes were simple, others were more complicated.

He repented of his long-standing habit of "framing the truth" to make himself and his department look better. For years he sold his corporate clients more technology than they needed, thinking that if they were foolish enough to fall for his sales pitch, too bad for them. Instead of trying to write the most lucrative contracts he could get away with, Ray worked hard to meet the real needs of his customers. The symbols of status that had meant so much to him became less and less important. He befriended the people he had ignored as he climbed the ladder of corporate success. He sought to rectify the workplace injustices that he condoned in the past. In short, he began following Jesus everywhere he went. The compartmentalized mix of secular values and religious piety that he had fostered for many years was no longer possible. He deliberately became more Christlike, and thus more humble, submissive, relational, loving, and truthful. And often when he prayed he knelt.

Upper Room Reflection

What do you make of John's detailed description of Jesus' actions?
How have you been taught to think about humility?
What impact does Jesus' example have on your work life?
How do you counter the world's bias against humility?

DAY 12

Divine Humility

"Jesus knew that the Father had put all things under his power, and that he had come from God and was returning to God; so he got up from the meal..." JOHN 13:3-4

JESUS' SELF-UNDERSTANDING IS IN tandem with his self-sacrifice. Compressed into a single sentence we have the heights and depths of the New Testament understanding of Christ. We resist identifying Jesus' divine nature with the Gospel of John 13:3 and his human nature with 13:4. "So he got up from the meal, took off his outer clothing, wrapped a towel around his waist. After that, he poured water into a basin and began to wash the disciples' feet..." There is no justification for dividing his nature up this way. He is fully God and fully human in a single being who is one with the Father.

In his exposition of 1 Corinthians 13, on love and humility, early American theologian Jonathan Edwards offered remarkable insights into the nature of Christlike humility. But he was emphatic on one point that I wish he had reconsidered. Edwards argued that "humility is not, and cannot be, an attribute of the divine nature." He reasoned as follows:

> God's nature is indeed infinitely opposite to pride, and yet humility cannot properly be predicted of him; for if it could, this would argue imperfection, which is impossible in God. God, who is infinite in excellence and glory, and infinitely above all things, cannot have any comparative meanness [inferiority], and of course cannot have any such comparative meanness to be sensible of, and therefore cannot be humble. But humility is an excellence proper to all created intelligent beings, for they are all infinitely little and mean before God, and most of them are in some way mean and low in comparison with some of their fellow-creatures.[1]

Edwards defined humility as "a habit of mind and heart corresponding to our comparative unworthiness and vileness before God." This definition is true but not complete. Humility belongs not only to our sinfulness, but also to our exalted status in Christ. Humility is defined not only negatively, but positively. Jesus humbled himself, knowing that the Father had put all things under his power. On bended knee, God preaches humility, a humility based on the righteousness, security, and self-esteem found in communion with the triune God. This grace-filled humility is inherent in the divine nature of Christ and belongs to us in Christ. If humility were an attribute derived only from the disciple's sinfulness, insecurities, and inadequacies, then humility would be rooted in our humiliation. But true humility corresponds to the confidence, authority, well-being, and self-esteem we have in Christ. The followers of Jesus are empowered to be humble. We have two good reasons to be humble. First, we are miserable sinners in need of God's grace. That reason is obvious. Second, we belong to God. We share in his glory, a more than sufficient reason for humility. Humility is rooted in our fallen condition *and* in our exalted status in Christ.

In the Bible, humility and glory are richly textured words. Their multifaceted meaning fits the proverbial two sides of the same coin. In Christian theology we cannot have one without the

---

1. Edwards, *Charity and Its Fruits*, 131.

other. There has never been a time that the glory of the triune God has existed apart from the humility of God. The fact that the Lamb was slain from the creation of the world affirms this truth (Rev 13:8). When Jesus laid aside his outer clothing, he knew he was "the image of the invisible God, the firstborn over all creation" (Col 1:15). He was conscious of his glorious destiny *and* his ignominious death. He understood his universal sovereignty *and* his path to the cross. He knew who he was *and* he knew the burden of our iniquity. He who made human feet was willing to stoop to wash them!

When Jesus deliberately dressed down, he dramatically portrayed his descent into humble service and sacrifice. The Creator on bended knee humbly served the creature and the caption under John's picture reads, "He now showed them the full extent of his love." This unique act, divine foot-washing, is not out of character, but absolutely consistent with the divine love that serves and sustains us every single moment. The God who kneels is an apt description of God's saving grace.

There is a far greater danger of reading too little into this picture than reading too much. Missionary theologian Lesslie Newbigin writes, "The foot-washing is a sign of that ultimate subversion of all human power and authority which took place when Jesus was crucified by the decision of the 'powers' that rule this present age."[2]

John's word choice syncs the Gospel narrative with this single act. When we read that Jesus *laid aside* his outer clothing, we are led back to the description of the good shepherd who *lays down* his life for the sheep. John draws a deliberate parallel between his high Christology and Jesus' path to the cross.

"The good shepherd *lays down* his life for the sheep. . . . Just as the Father knows me and I know the Father—and I *lay down* my life for the sheep. . . . The reason my Father loves me is that I *lay down* my life—only to take it up again. No one takes it from me, but I *lay it down* of my own accord. I have authority to *lay it down*

---

2. Newbigin, *The Light Has Come*, 168.

and authority to take it up again. This command I received from my Father" (John 10:11, 15, 17, 18).

These two acts, *laying aside* and *laying down*, form one consistent testimony to divine humility. Jesus laid aside his divine nature and his outer garment in order to lay down his life for us. This is the humility that inspires our discipleship; the humility rooted in our exalted status in Christ; the humility based not on our fallen human condition but on God's redemptive provision. Christ in us, the hope of glory; Christ in us, the hope of humility. This is the compelling, compassionate humility that unites self-understanding and self-sacrifice. A disciple, wrote Dallas Willard, "is anyone whose ultimate goal is to live as Jesus would live if he were in their place."[3]

Upper Room Reflection

Why is humility a divine attribute?

If you think your Lord and Savior humbled himself, what impact does that have on you?

In what sense is humility the evidence of daily cross-bearing?

How does *laying aside* and *laying down* form one continuous act of discipleship?

---

3. Ortberg, "Dallas Willard."

DAY 13

No Reputation

"He made himself a man of no reputation, taking on the very nature of a servant." PHILIPPIANS 2:7, KJV

THERE IS A REMARKABLE parallel between Jesus' deliberate action in John 13 and Christ's self-emptying in Philippians 2. Although there are few verbal parallels, "the parallels in thought and in the progression of action are startling."[1] Philippians 2 is Paul's commentary on John's understanding of Christ, and they are in perfect harmony.

John 13	Philippians 2
1. Lays aside his outer clothes.	1. Lays aside his divine nature.
2. Takes a towel and wraps it around himself.	2. Takes the form of a slave.
3. He humbled himself and washed the disciples' feet.	3. He humbled himself and became obedient to death.
4. When he finished, he returned to his place.	4. When he finished, God exalted him to the highest place.
5. You call me "Teacher" and "Lord" and rightly so.	5. Every tongue confesses Jesus Christ is Lord.

1. Hawthorne, *Philippians*, 78.

The theological continuum stretches from the self-emptying of Christ in the incarnation to Jesus' selfless act of washing the disciples' feet. It is all of one truth. The reality of the incarnation and the atonement converge in an everyday act of true discipleship. The Apostle Paul explains the motivation for embracing this humility in entirely positive terms.

> If you have any encouragement from being united with Christ, if any comfort from his love, if any common sharing in the Spirit, if any tenderness and compassion, then make my joy complete by being like-minded, having the same love, being one in spirit and of one mind. Do nothing out of selfish ambition or vain conceit. Rather, in humility value others above yourselves, not looking to your own interests but each of you to the interests of the others. In your relationships with one another, have the same attitude of mind Christ Jesus had . . . (Phil 2:1–5).

Jesus' self-awareness and self-sacrifice are the foundation for the believer's self-understanding and self-sacrifice. Since we know who we are in Christ, we can experience the freedom and liberty to give ourselves in Christlike service. When Scott Rodin stepped down from the presidency of Eastern Baptist Theological Seminary in 2001, he had a confession to make. "I was wrong," he admitted. "I was wrong in my understanding and preconceived notions of leadership in Christian ministry. I was wrong in my expectations of others and myself. And I was wrong in my motivations, which may be the hardest thing to admit."[2] When he became president he sensed that he was well-prepared, strongly motivated, and truly called. The biblical verse that epitomized his leadership ideal was the prophet Nathan's directive to King David, "Whatever you have in mind, go ahead and do it, for the Lord is with you" (2 Sam 7:3). Now a different verse epitomizes his understanding of leadership. He quotes Paul's description of the incarnate Son of God. Paul says of Jesus, "he made himself a man of no reputation, taking on the very nature of a servant" (Phil 2:7, KJV).

---

2. Rodin, "Notes from the Field," 105.

DAY 13

Rodin explains: "The verse does not say that Jesus became a man of bad reputation, or questionable reputation, but simply of 'no' reputation. That is, reputation, image, prestige, prominence, power, and other trappings of leadership were not only devalued, they were purposefully dismissed. . . . In reflecting on these past five years, I have come to believe that true Christian leadership is an ongoing, disciplined practice of becoming a person of no reputation, and thus, becoming more like Christ in this unique way."[3]

"I have left my years in the presidency with a dramatically transformed understanding of godly leadership," concludes Rodin. "In the end, our work as leaders is all about Lordship. Before it is about vision-casting or risk-taking or motivating others or building teams or communicating or strategic planning, it is about Lordship. Where Jesus is singularly and absolutely Lord of our life, we will seek to be like him and him only. . . . And as we do, we will be transformed into the likeness of Christ, becoming leaders of no reputation."[4]

John's description of foot-washing humility and eucharistic intimacy stand in iconic opposition to the human propensity for recognition and honor. If our Lord and Savior emptied himself and laid aside his outer garment and wrapped a towel around his waist to wash the disciples' feet, maybe the church has lost something when the archbishop dresses in elaborate vestments or when the trendy pastor shows off his tattoos. The archbishop wears a purple ring on his finger and a heavy gold cross around his neck, and the street-cool, MTV-generation pastor wears his skinny jeans and bicep-revealing T-shirt. Neither seem to grasp the Jesus way. High-church leaders wear garments inherited from pagan priests and cool dude pastors mimic rappers and models. Appearance is everything.

Now picture the eloquent archbishop and the hipster pastor sitting in the upper room. Their feet are washed by Jesus. Their egos deflated; their souls humbled. Neither liturgical fastidiousness nor

---

3. Ibid., 106.
4. Ibid., 119.

laid-back spirituality is on their minds. All protocol and performance ceased when they walked into the upper room. But that's not only true for them, it's true for *me*. No one can "fake it to make it" in the upper room. All of our silly self-centeredness is uncovered. My pale blue button-down ego is exposed.

The "open secret" for true reverence and real authenticity lies right before our eyes in the deeply personal and down-to-earth practical example of Jesus. God on bended knee strips down and washes the dirty feet of his disciples as a precursor to his death on the cross for our atonement. Yet for some reason this is not the kind of seriousness and intimacy we have come to embrace. Sadly, we expect something different. We pull back from the Jesus way.

In *The Outpost: An Untold Story of American Valor*, Jake Tapper of CNN traces First Lieutenant Ben Keating's self-sacrificing philosophy of leadership to Jesus. As a kid, Keating spent hours reading his copy of David C. Cook's *The Picture Bible*, a 766-page comic-book version of the entire Bible. Keating was particularly impressed with Jesus washing the feet of his disciples. Tapper quotes the passage verbatim:

> Peter: "No, Lord, I'm not good enough to have you wait on me!"
>
> Jesus: "If you do not let me serve you, Peter, you will have no place in my kingdom."

After Jesus has washed all the disciples' feet, he sits down at the table again.

> Jesus: "If I, your lord and master, have served you, you should do the same for one another. The servant is not greater than his master."

> Tapper concludes, "And that was Ben Keating. 'You don't ever ask your soldiers to do anything you wouldn't do,' he would say. 'You have to serve them to get the best leadership out of them.' Other soldiers might have come to the same conclusion in their own ways, but it was a safe bet

that Keating was the only member of the 10th Mountain Division who'd brought with him to Afghanistan a copy of *The Confessions of Saint Augustine*—in Latin."[5]

When Keating received orders at Combat Outpost Kamdesh to send back to the main base an eight-ton light medium tactical vehicle (LMTV) he took it upon himself to drive the truck. In spite of a standing order that officers were not to drive vehicles, Keating deemed the operation too risky and foolish to ask anyone else to drive the truck. The only way back to the main base was along a dangerous mountain road running along a steep ravine. Although headquarters was advised repeatedly that the road had deteriorated to the point that even a much lighter seven-foot-wide Humvee could not safely make it on the road, the orders stood. Since convoys were repeatedly ambushed along this road, the trip took place under the cover of darkness. "'It is stupid,' Keating agreed. 'And it's dangerous. So I'm going to drive.'"

On a sharp curve the weight of the eight-ton vehicle was too much for the road and it gave way. The LMTV slid over the edge and crashed and tumbled down the mountain until it came to stop on the rocks in the river below. Keating was thrown from the vehicle and suffered massive injuries. In the end, First Lieutenant Keating's decision to drive the LMTV proved fatal, but it was a decision that also proved his faithfulness. He made the sacrifice because of his commitment to Christ and the Jesus way. This American soldier died in eastern Afghanistan a true servant of Jesus Christ. He never got over the example of Jesus that he first learned as kid reading David C. Cook's *The Picture Bible*.

Upper Room Reflection

How significant is the parallel between John 13 and Philippians 2 for shaping the Christian life?

What can we do to curb our appetite for self-recognition?

---

5. Tapper, *The Outpost*, 64–65.

What makes self-emptying discipleship difficult to learn and practice?

How did Ben Keating follow his Lord?

DAY 14

Logos Logic

"Lord, are you going to wash my feet?" JOHN 13:6

AUGUSTINE INSISTED THAT PETER was the first to have his feet washed.[1] John's narrative implies otherwise. As Jesus moved down the row of disciples, Peter could see it coming. He was next, and when Jesus knelt down to wash his feet, Peter objected, "Lord, are you going to wash my feet?" The impression is given of Peter spluttering in astonishment and incomprehension, "Master, you . . . my . . . !"[2] His delayed timing seemed calculated to prove his superiority. His exaggerated shock and definitive "no" was premeditated. Peter was emphatic; Jesus was not going to wash his feet.

Why do we insist on defending the honor of Christ in ways that contradict his words and actions? Sincerity is a poor substitute for faithfulness. To say that we mean well does not justify our actions. Pride and power lurk behind our vain practices and religious habits. As with Peter, what is done ostensibly to honor Christ may only put the ego on display. There is a willfulness about Peter's "never" that I hear echo in my own soul.

1. Augustine, "Homilies on the Gospel of John," 301.
2. Beasley-Murray, *John*, 233.

Peter interpreted Jesus' actions as embarrassing and demeaning. Foot-washing was beneath the office of the Messiah. Peter wanted Jesus to act like a hero instead of a lowly servant. He may have wondered if the hostility and death threats had finally gotten to Jesus. Who knows what Peter was thinking? Peter was literally and emotionally looking down on Jesus. The negative feelings he felt in that moment may have been akin to Judas' resentment of Jesus. No one wants to follow a leader who exhibits behavior considered demeaning. Acting more like Jesus' advisor than his disciple, Peter seems to want Jesus to snap out of it and play the role of the messiah as Peter understood and envisioned it.

Embracing Jesus' redemptive trajectory is difficult for all disciples, not just Peter. We get the confession right, but fail to grasp the costly commitment. We freely confess, "You are the Christ, the Son of the living God," but then take Jesus aside and rebuke him (Matt 16:15–23). Dogmatically we whisper, "Never, Lord!" We object to the path of discipleship that Jesus himself laid down. We stand between Jesus and the cross, slow to understand the meaning of the gospel and resistant to the practical realities inherent in confessing Christ as Lord. It is not only the secular agendas and pagan lifestyles that stand in the way of knowing Christ and becoming like Jesus, it is our own well-meaning religious habits.

Peter's "Never, Lord!" represents the culture-bound Christian who proclaims the deity of Christ but unwittingly resists the practical meaning of Spirit-led confession and cruciform commitment. Peter lacked the humility to listen to Jesus. In his enthusiasm and zeal he refused to accept Jesus' explanation of the Messiah's suffering and death. Like Peter, we may hear the Spirit but end up in Satan's camp. Jesus rebuked Peter, "Get behind me, Satan!" (Matt 16:23; Mark 8:33). It is chilling to realize that we can be so close to Jesus yet get it so wrong.

Jesus emphasized that the life of discipleship was the true follow-up to a Spirit-led confession: "If anyone would come after me, he must deny himself and take up his cross and follow me" (Matt 16:24). Insight means action, and action leads to understanding. There is a lively exchange between confession and commitment

DAY 14

that authenticates confession and purifies commitment. We cannot follow Jesus any way we please. His glory is defined in a specific way. "If you love me," Jesus said, "keep my commands" (John 14:15). We are led by his example through the power of his Spirit. In the upper room Jesus showed us how to do theology on our knees in a humility based on the cross. In spite of his experience at Caesarea Philippi, Peter failed to understand the relationship between Spirit-led confession and costly commitment. He defended the office of Messiah in his own way, according to his own expectations, in spite of what Jesus said or did.

When Jesus came to Peter on bended knee with towel and basin, Peter asked, "Lord, are you going to wash my feet?" Was his tone inquisitive or indignant? Jesus replied, "You do not realize now what I am doing, but later you will understand." This should have checked Peter's pride, but Peter adamantly answered back, "*No,* you shall *never* wash my feet." Peter's "no" and "never" are emphatic. The other disciples may acquiesce and passively receive Jesus' service, but not Peter. He was determined to prove his loyalty to Christ in spite of Jesus.

Foot-washing is a metaphor for what Christ calls us to do for others. The work of the servant may take many forms that are perceived by the recipient as unnecessary or demeaning. When parents serve their children and teachers serve their students in Christlike ways, they may run into Peter-like resistance. In the home, parental foot-washing serves the child with selfless love. In church, pedagogical foot-washing asks the soul-searching questions that go well beyond cognitive memorization. One's private life is fair game for spiritual formation and the workplace comes knowingly under the realm of Christ's Lordship. Parenting is the work of disciple making. In either case the Christlike servant intrudes into personal space in ways that may strike the recipient as unwarranted and bothersome. Humble love is humiliating to the unsuspecting ego. Due to our sinful nature, the costly love of parents and mentors can be misunderstood as demeaning. Recipients of Jesus-inspired foot-washing may perceive such love as a threat to their self-respect. They may recoil on "spiritual" grounds and respond like Peter with an emphatic "Never!"

Upper Room Reflection

How does your natural bent run counter to what Christ wants you to do?

Why do we insist on honoring Christ according to our own agenda?

What made Peter's resistance well-intentioned but misguided?

What have you had to unlearn in order to follow Jesus?

DAY 15

Humility and Humiliation

"You shall never wash my feet." JOHN 13:8

THE KNEELING MASTER SAID "yes" to the disciple. The seated disciple said "no" to Jesus. Peter felt his "no" was for his Master's own good. He sought to rescue Jesus from this unwarranted humiliation and defend his self-respect. The outspoken, impetuous disciple had not yet grasped the redemptive trajectory leading to the cross. He failed to embrace the humility of God.

In the upper room there is tension between humility and humiliation. These two realities are as opposite as good and evil. Humility is a spiritual discipline rooted in the cross. It is an intentional commitment of the will in relationship to God and others. It is a chosen and cultivated quality of character that matures and deepens with our experience of Christ. Humility is a surrender of our will to the commands of God. The apostle's exhortation, "Have this mind in you which was also in Christ Jesus," calls for an intentional and resolute self-emptying (Phil 2:5).

Humiliation, on the other hand, is the feeling of shame, inadequacy, and disappointment that comes from our sinful self-reliance. Humility is the chosen awareness of our needy dependence on the mercy and wisdom of God. Humiliation involves trusting in ourselves; humility involves trusting in God. Humiliation rejects God; humility bows before God. Humiliation leads to discouragement, disorientation, and despair; humility leads to hope. Humiliation thrives on self-promotion; humility frees us from the pressure to make a name for ourselves. Humiliation is our enemy, we feel it in our soul; but humility is our friend, whether we know it or not. For there is no other way to deal with humiliation than through humility.

The clash between humility and humiliation in the upper room continues today in the defensive postures of believers who seek to rescue the gospel from the Jesus way. Jesus, first on his knees and then on the cross, disorients the well-meaning Christian who consumes Jesus as a spiritual additive. We don't understand the redemptive strategy that intends to turn our world upside down. We bargained for a saved soul, not a transformed life. When we came to Christ, we didn't count on Jesus' kingdom priorities. We thought "the first will be last and the last first" was a nice slogan, not a reality that would change our world. We never intended to make the poor and needy our priority, nor did we expect to reach out to the outcast and the outsider. We thought our goal was to climb the ladder of Christian success, but in the upper room we learn that Jesus has a different agenda in mind.

The exchange between Jesus and Peter is reflected today in our resistance to the foot-washing mission of the church. We are fine with the doctrine of the cross. Cognitive explanations and conceptual descriptions are satisfying. But the redemptive trajectory of the cross worked out in our personal lives is often confusing and messy. We like the idea of vision-casting excitement and entrepreneurial church growth, but the daily grind of cross-bearing is another matter. The Christian faith is not a set of good ideas: it is the truth that redeems and revolutionizes. When you are undergoing chemotherapy or your spouse walks out on you, the gospel becomes what it has been all along: a matter of life and death.

Like Peter, we sit in judgment of the Jesus way. We look down on the Lord Jesus who is on his knees washing our feet. Honestly, we think that we know how to run the Christian life better than Jesus. Success-minded Christian leaders defend their self-help strategies in a manner reminiscent of Peter's defense of the Messiah. Peter's preconceived notion of a nationalistic messiah runs counter to the truth of the Suffering Servant and the Lamb of God. Moving from a political messiah to the crucified and risen Savior of the world was difficult for Peter, just as moving from our misguided messianic notions may be difficult for us.

Helmet Thielicke was a pastor in post-World War II Hamburg, Germany. His ministry and preaching were influenced by the well-known nineteenth-century London preacher Charles Spurgeon. Thielicke was impressed by Spurgeon's rejection of "high-minded Christian pragmatism." He wrote: "It was not the aim of [Spurgeon's] preaching to show people that their life would be easier if they accepted the gospel; that it would solve their problems; that their civilization would perish without Christianity; that the state and society need religion; that the Christian social ethic is absolutely indispensable; that the world order needs Christian foundations; that all the misery of modern man comes from secularism; that if our world is to endure there must be a renaissance of the Christian West, and so on."[1]

Thielicke argued that Spurgeon was not trying to sell society on a practical religious plan. His aim was to bring people to the foot of the cross. The gospel is all about salvation through the cross of Christ. In the upper room Peter fixated on his worldly logic. What little he understood of the redemptive trajectory, that span from foot-washing to crucifixion, he found humiliating, not humbling. He couldn't get his head and heart around the Logos logic, that humility that led to God's gracious redemptive provision. If we find the God who kneels humiliating rather than humbling, we will always end up catering to our own wishes. Jesus didn't get down on his knees to make life easier for people or to take back America or save Western civilization. He got down on his knees

---

1. Thielicke, *Encounter with Spurgeon*, 42.

to show us the redemptive love of God. Worldly logic will always clash with Logos logic.

Upper Room Reflection

How do you distinguish between humility and humiliation?

If humility is grounded in the humility of God, how does that change you?

What political and nationalistic expectations should Christians develop?

Have you ever experienced the clash between worldly logic and Logos logic?

DAY 16

Patience

"Unless I wash you, you have no part with me." JOHN 13:8

IF YOU WERE JESUS, and Peter had said to you, "No, you shall never wash my feet," what would you have done? I think some of us might have said, "Fine, have it your way," and moved on to the next disciple. My patience can be on a short fuse. I'm too eager to bypass the slightly resistant or reticent disciple. If I could be as patient with others as Christ is patient with me, my ministry would be more faithful and fruitful.

IN DEVOTIONS ONE MORNING I read from Luke: "If anyone would come after me, he must deny himself and take up his cross and follow me. For whoever wants to save his life will lose it, but whoever loses his life for me will save it" (Luke 9:23–24). I was a senior at Wheaton College at the time and working on plans for the coming year. After devotions I intended to write to Dr. Paul Han, who had invited me to teach at Chung Yuan Christian College in Taiwan come fall. I had it all worked out in my sophomoric spiritual mind.

I'd thank him for his gracious invitation and tell him that I'd come in January, not September. I'd be there for the second semester. My excuse was that I wanted to work on my MA degree, but my real reason was that I was in love with Virginia, who was later to become my wife. I couldn't imagine being apart from her for the summer and then flying off to Taiwan to teach for a year.

The only obstacle that morning to *dictating* to the Lord and Dr. Han *my terms* of commitment was the Word of God. There I was, sitting at my little desk innocently reading about taking up my cross and following Jesus. I was reflecting naively on Luke's description of wannabe disciples who so easily excused themselves from following Jesus. Like them, I was ready with my lame excuse, "I will follow you, Lord, *but . . .*" when suddenly it hit me. I was about to do the same thing! Of course Dr. Han wanted me in the fall, that's when teachers start the school year. I had prayed for weeks that the Lord would work out this opportunity and lead Dr. Han to invite me, but when it came time to accept the assignment, I was as willful as Peter. I will never forget that particular devotional time. I guess that's why I'm sharing it with you forty years later. The meaning of the Word struck me with exceptional force. So, that morning I wrote to Dr. Han to say that I'd be there in the fall.

Jesus worked with Peter patiently, as he works with you and me. He reasoned with Peter calmly, "Unless I wash you, you have no part with me" (John 13:8). The patience and humility of the Lord Jesus in the upper room is the prime example of how we should lead when we are surrounded by tension and confusion. That night, all the positive action belonged to Jesus. He served on bended knee, taught at the table, warned the weak, and in love, exposed his betrayer. He mentored Peter, like he disciples us, in love and wisdom. Like a parent with a toddler, Jesus helps us to take "baby steps" along the path of discipleship.

Every kind of evil surrounded this table fellowship: hatred, pride, self-righteousness, deception, betrayal, and denial. The upper room was no retreat from the world, the flesh, and the devil. But in the midst of all this high stress and deep anxiety, Jesus

DAY 16

remained calm. We are not surprised. But note carefully the many ways that Jesus, through his calm spirit and patient direction, kept the evening focused on faithfulness. There was never any doubt as to who was in charge. Everything happened in an orderly fashion. The timing, location, and preparation for celebrating the Passover meal were under Jesus' direction. He saved his anguished thoughts for Gethsemane; he reserved his agony of soul for communion with the Father. In the upper room with his disciples, he was calm and patient, attending to their real needs. His leadership prevailed in the midst of the storm. Jesus persisted in loving Peter, patiently persuading and preparing him for what was coming.

Upper Room Reflection

How is Jesus' patience with Peter a model for our patience with others?

Have you ever prided yourself on being patient with God, only to realize that it is God who is patient with you?

If you had been Peter, what would you have learned from this encounter with Jesus?

How can we effectively mentor younger disciples?

DAY 17

Clean Feet and a Pure Heart

"Those who have had a bath need only to wash their feet; their whole body is clean." JOHN 13:10

IN HIS MEDITATION ON love, the nineteenth-century Danish Christian thinker Søren Kierkegaard distinguished between loving the people we actually see versus a high-flying love that is always waiting for the right person to love. He compared airy love to actual love. He based his spiritual direction on 1 John: "We love because he first loved us. If we say we love God yet hate a brother or sister, we are liars. For if we do not love a fellow believer, whom we have seen, we cannot love God, whom we have not seen" (1 John 4:19–20).

Kierkegaard reasoned that our duty is not to find "the lovable object" but to find the person before us lovable. Actual love, loving the person before us, is always concrete and often sacrificial. "Truth takes a firm step," says Kierkegaard, "and for that reason sometimes a difficult one, too." The opposite of actual love is a theory of love focused on the ideal. "Delusion is always floating; for that reason it sometimes appears quite light and spiritual, because

DAY 17

it is so airy."[1] We are to love our children, coworkers, neighbors, and strangers, not because we have chosen to love them, but because Christ calls us to love them. Peter was a challenging person to love, but Jesus loved him deeply. For Kierkegaard, when real love is shown, "truth takes a firm step."

My hunch is that none of us need to look very far to find a challenging person to love. A day after rereading Kierkegaard on love, I received an accusatory email from a church member. His criticism against me and others was deep-seated and meanspirited. My immediate impulse was to fire back an angry email to set the record straight and defend myself. But Kierkegaard's *intrusive* reminder to love as Christ loved was stuck in my mind. I remember wishing it wasn't.

We never have far to look for a person to love who is impossible to love apart from the grace of God. Actual love is for the real people with whom we must deal daily. Airy love is a fine-sounding theory filled with ethereal possibilities. The gospel is rooted in the former. Dirty feet and dirty souls are linked and Christ's love meets us at every point along the span of human need.

In the Gospel of John, Jesus is the link between the old creation and the new creation, between baptism with water and baptism with the Holy Spirit, between the old temple in Jerusalem and the new temple of his body, between natural birth and the new birth, between physical water and the living water, between physical healing and spiritual healing, between the letter of the Law and the living Word, between ordinary bread and the bread of life, between natural life and the light of the world, between physical blindness and true sight, and between death and life. This is more than a metaphoric bridge to significance; Christ holds creation and redemption together. He actively sustains the entire physical and spiritual universe moment by moment. By the time we get to the upper room the disciples have been thoroughly exposed to Jesus' understanding of the world and his unique redemptive responsibility, but they fail to grasp his significance.

---

1. Kierkegaard, *Works of Love*, 158–61.

The connection between dirty feet and the divine atonement is in the mind of Jesus. He only alludes to it, exposing the tip of the iceberg as it were. He slants the truth at such a sharp angle, we might wonder how anyone could pick up on it. But Jesus can afford to be oblique, because the connection between physical cleansing and the holiness of God is deeply embedded in Jewish culture. He is telling the truth slanted, as Emily Dickinson would say, because it is a truth that "must dazzle gradually."[2]

An Old Testament theology of clean and unclean forms the theological backdrop of this upper room picture. Legal explicitness on ceremonial and ritual purity is covered extensively in Leviticus. These laws established the standard for cleanness and covered prohibited foods and exposure to external contaminants (bodily emissions, skin diseases, dead bodies, and certain acts). But even more important was the symbolic connection between outward physical purity as prescribed by the law and the righteous holiness of God. Out of devotion to Yahweh the people of God followed the purity protocol.

Jesus taps into this symbolic connection between physical cleansing and spiritual cleansing. His foot-washing is symbolic of another kind of cleansing. It is a pointer to the cleansing he will achieve for us through his redemptive death. What is missing in Jesus' parable is any analogical bridge between ritual temple cleansing and spiritual cleansing. He figuratively leaped over the symbolic liturgical connection and rooted the message in the profane, everyday world of simple hospitality. This may be more important than we realize. There was plenty of opportunity to draw out the Old Testament connection between ritual purity and sacrificial cleansing, but Jesus didn't do that. Instead, he turned the upper room into the most holy place. He made his theological connection with the atonement through foot-washing rather than ritual cleansing. Jesus used ordinary foot-washing to illustrate the soul-cleansing power of his sacrificial death. As it was with Peter and the disciples so it is with us: foot-washing love points to the

---

2. Dickinson, *The Complete Poems*, 507.

cleansing power of Jesus' blood. This is the love that is actual, not airy. "Truth takes a firm step."

Upper Room Reflection

What people or situations in your life test the authenticity of your love?

Why is "talking-head" Christianity unsatisfying?

Do you think the disciples understood the connection between physical cleansing and spiritual cleansing?

What is the relationship between Jesus' atoning sacrifice and "foot-washing" acts of love?

DAY 18

Holy of Holies

"Unless I was you, you have no part with me."
"Do you understand what I have done for you?"
JOHN 13:8,12

EVERYTHING DEPENDS ON THE "I" when Jesus says, "Unless I wash you . . ." This simple assertion depends on nothing less than the highest understanding of Christ. The deep truth of the atonement depends on Jesus being fully God and fully human. This singular magisterial "I" corresponds to the seven "I am" sayings in John. Jesus transposed the action of foot-washing into a parable of the atonement centered on himself. He is the one upon whom this parable of sacrificial love turns. The soul-cleansing power of the atonement is symbolized in foot-washing. Jesus washed his disciples' feet with water, but in a matter of hours he would shed his blood on the cross for the remission of our sins. The author of Hebrews expressed it this way:

> Since we have confidence to enter the Most Holy Place by the blood of Jesus, by a new and living way opened for us through the curtain of his body, and since we have a great priest over the house of God, let us draw near to

DAY 18

> God with a sincere heart in full assurance of faith, having our hearts sprinkled to cleanse us from a guilty conscience and having our bodies washed with pure water (Heb 10:19–22).

On the night that Jesus washed feet and broke bread in the upper room, he transformed the upper room into the holy of holies. He gave the disciples a sign of his redemptive cleansing and a promise of his partnership through his death and resurrection. Outward foot-washing pointed to inward soul cleansing by his blood. He miraculously turned water to wine at the wedding feast and he sacrificially turned water into blood at the cross. John expressed it graphically in his short letter when he wrote, "the blood of Jesus cleanses us from all sin" (1 John 1:7). In the book of Revelation, he pictured the great company of worshipers in heaven, who "have washed their robes and made them white in the blood of the Lamb" (Rev 7:14).

Dr. Paul Brand and author Philip Yancey wrote an extraordinary article entitled, "Blood: The Miracle of Cleansing."[1] They showed how the physiological function of blood corresponds perfectly to the theological meaning of blood in the New Testament. What blood does in our physical bodies is analogous to what the blood of Jesus does in the body of Christ. Blood literally cleanses the body of toxins and waste and serves as a metaphor for the cleansing promised in the new covenant. When Jesus instituted the Last Supper, he said, "This is my blood of the covenant, which is poured out for many for the forgiveness of sins" (Matt 26:28). William Cowper's hymn makes for both good theology and good biology: "There is a fountain filled with blood drawn from Emmanuel's veins; And sinners, plunged beneath that flood, lose all their guilty stains . . ."

Jesus' response to Peter's ill-conceived "no" was decisive. Jesus said, "Unless I wash you, you have no part with me." In a second Peter flipped his position. He went from foot-dragging resistance to cheerleading enthusiasm: "Then, Lord, not just my feet but my

---

1. Brand and Yancey, "Blood: The Miracle of Cleansing."

hands and my head as well!" To paraphrase Peter, "You've sold me, Jesus, I'm in it all the way!" But Peter's enthusiasm was not all that helpful. His response compounds his failure to understand what Jesus is saying and what the Master is about to accomplish on the cross. One suspects that Peter was motivated out of personal loyalty rather than his need for soul cleansing. He is the picture of a well-intentioned but clueless believer who fails to comprehend the truth. Peter substitutes an enthusiastic and shallow interpretation of what it means to follow Jesus. His emotional and relational experience is not grounded in understanding but in the feeling of the moment. He had an existential reason, but he still had not grasped the redemptive power of Jesus' shed blood.

Regardless of the situation, Peter seems intent on drawing attention to himself. Of all the disciples, he presents himself as the most loyal and the most enthusiastic. Yet for all of his bravado he pays little attention to Jesus. He is caught up in his own reality. First, he resists the Lord's overture to wash his feet. Then, he is obnoxious about being the most enthusiastic: "Not just my feet but my hands and my head as well!" Peter's instinctive reactions, like my own, tend to be wrong.

Precisely at this point his spirituality is typical of many well-meaning believers who insist on being in the emotional spotlight. "Spiritual theology," writes Eugene Peterson, " is the discipline and art of training us into a full and mature participation in Jesus' story while at the same time preventing us from taking over the story."[2] Peter wants to take over the story, but the story is not about him. Nevertheless, Jesus deals with Peter and the rest of us in love and patience.

Upper Room Reflection

How does Jesus' foot-washing object lesson transform the upper room into the holy of holies?

What makes physical blood work as a redemptive analogy?

2. Peterson, *Christ Plays in Ten Thousand Places*, 199.

DAY 18

Why is Peter's reaction a warning to us all?

How have you been tempted to make the Christian life all about you?

DAY 19

Foot-washing vs. Hand-washing

"Those who have had a bath need only to wash their feet; their whole body is clean. And you are clean, though not every one of you." JOHN 13:10

JESUS CALMLY MOVES THE conversation forward. While he is still on his knees, Jesus blows Judas's cover, but in the most limited and indirect way possible. The reason for exposing Judas in the upper room may have been to assure that there would be no confusion among the disciples later regarding Judas's spiritual condition. Judas experienced the "object lesson" of cleansing, but he was unwilling to receive and believe in Jesus. After Judas left, Jesus reassured the rest of the disciples with these words: "You are already clean because of the word I have spoken to you" (John 15:3). Judas participated fully in an outward relationship with Jesus, but inwardly he refused to enter into true faith and trust in Christ. Judas represents those who participate in baptism and the Lord's Supper, but never enter into a relationship with Christ. They experience the "object lesson" of the atonement, but they themselves have not received Christ.

DAY 19

In the Passion Narrative, there is one more reference to cleansing that draws our attention. Less than twenty-four hours after Jesus washed the feet of the disciples, he stood before Pilate at the Praetorium. The Roman governor sat on his judge's seat overlooking a large and angry crowd. The religious leaders had turned public sentiment against Jesus. The crowd was on the verge of riot, and Pilate, adept at mob control, exerted his political skills. Since it was the governor's custom to release a prisoner during the Passover festival, he offered the crowd a choice: Jesus Barabbas, the terrorist, or Jesus, the teacher (Matt 27:16). Persuaded by the scribes and Pharisees, the crowd shouted, "Barabbas!" Turning to Jesus, Pilate asked, "Why? What crime has he committed?" But the crowd shouted all the louder, "Crucify him! Crucify him!" It is scandalous that the one who healed the sick, loved the outcast, and the transformed the corrupt should be sentenced to die by Roman crucifixion. Jesus was chosen to die a hideously cruel death by popular vote.

Pilate called for a basin of water to be brought, and he "washed his hands in front of the crowd" (Matt 27:24). In a theatrical gesture, he dramatically washed his hands of the whole affair. The work of our hands is a figure of speech signifying human action. The psalmist used the figure as an outward expression of inner purity when he said, "Surely in vain I have kept my heart pure and have washed my hands in innocence" (Ps 73:13). But in Pilate's case, the empty gesture covered up the obvious fact that he was shirking his responsibility and ignoring his moral duty. Under Roman law it was his responsibility to adjudicate justice, but he gave in to mob rule for the sake of political expediency. Pilate added propaganda to his pantomime when he said to the hushed crowd, "I am innocent of this man's blood. It is your responsibility!" (Matt 27:24).

In your mind's eye, picture in split frame Jesus on bended knee, washing the disciples' feet, and Pilate, seated on the judgment seat, washing his hands. The two contrasting pictures symbolize the two types of cleansing available to us. We can receive the cleansing that only God can provide, or we can insist on proclaiming our innocence in the face of our sin. We can receive mercy from God or we can manipulate our conscience for the sake of public relations.

Upper Room Reflection

How is it possible to have full outward participation with Jesus but no inward relationship?

If the role of the disciple is to follow the Lord, do we have what it takes to get on our knees before those we seek to serve and to stand before corrupt, self-serving authorities?

How have you experienced the pressure to follow the crowd?

What is the difference between receiving God's grace and giving ourselves grace?

DAY 20

Deliberate Speech

"You also should wash one another's feet." JOHN 13:14

A MINI-COURSE IN DISCIPLESHIP follows the foot-washing parable. Conveyed in a mere six verses, the brevity, breadth, and depth of Jesus' training in discipleship is astonishing. We can draw from this well of truth forever and never run dry. In a single paragraph (John 13:12–17) Jesus offers a step-by-step tutorial in teaching excellence. He guides every believing pastor, parent, professor, and person in what it means to follow the Teacher and Lord. The way Jesus was with the disciples is the way we ought to be with one another.

"When he had finished washing their feet, he put on his clothes and returned to his place." John's simple transition invites our meditation on the relationship between humility and authority. "When he had *finished* . . ." is the prelude to the final word from the cross, when Jesus said, "It is *finished*." Foot-washing and the cross form a continuum stretching from one end of discipleship to another. All believers are called to serve as Jesus did along that continuum. This is where we find our place in the grand scheme of things. It is not up to us to brand the gospel with our image, but to teach the gospel "in accordance with the truth that is in Jesus" (Eph 4:21). Our strategies of communication follow Jesus' foot-washing modus operandi.

Foot-washing humility and Word of God authority belong together. This is the combination that Jesus chose, not only for himself, but for all of his followers. The two are inseparable and neither is sufficient apart from the other. This is a distinctive form of humility, not to be confused with conventional niceness and gestures of goodwill. Christian humility, insofar as it is a humility derived from Jesus, is different from any other kind of humility. Foot-washing humility refuses to bow the knee to Baal or kowtow to Caesar or give in to religious pride. H. R. Niebuhr called it a kind of "proud humility and humble pride" because "the humility of Christ is not the moderation of keeping one's exact place in the scale of being, but rather that of absolute dependence on God and absolute trust in Him, with the consequent ability to remove mountains. The secret of the meekness and the gentleness of Christ lies in his relation to God."[1]

Jonathan Edwards warned that "not every show and appearance of humility will stand the test of the gospel." The examples that "fall short of the reality," included "an affected humility" that confuses an emotional disposition of "natural low-spiritedness" and a character "wanting in manliness" with authentic self-sacrificing humility. "There is a counterfeit kind of humility, wrought by the delusions of Satan," warned Edwards, one that is the polar opposite of "the meek and lowly and crucified Jesus."[2]

The best context for authoritative spiritual direction, whether it be formal preaching or table conversation, is humble hands-on service. *After he had finished washing their feet*, Jesus assumed his place at the table. He put on his street clothes—not a white chasuble and pastoral stole, but his ordinary attire, the kind worn by fishermen and carpenters. Humility was his vestment. Truth

---

1. Niebuhr, *Christ and Culture*, 27.
2. Edwards, *Charity and Its Fruits*, 152–53.

was his authority and persuasion. Character was his platform. In the spirit of Jesus' humility, the Apostle Peter's spiritual direction comes to mind: "*Clothe yourselves in humility* toward one another, because 'God opposes the proud but gives grace to the humble.' Humble yourselves, therefore, under God's mighty hand, that he may lift you up in due time" (1 Pet 5:5–6).

Preachers who say the gospel entitles us to live our best life now are mistaken. We cannot say Jesus suffered in our place so we don't have to suffer, so we can be successful. We must not confuse the vicarious atonement with vicarious suffering. In Christ, self-identity and self-sacrifice are linked. Divine authority and divine humility are fully integrated. "He put on his clothes and returned to his place" (John 13:12). He assumed his rightful place as Teacher and Lord. Humble service and spiritual authority go together. We have emphasized that Jesus "knew that the Father had put all things under his power, and that he had come from God and was returning to God" (John 13:3). Humility and authority are inseparable.

"What we suffer from today," G. K. Chesterton wrote, "is humility in the wrong place." Humility has moved from ambition to conviction. "A man was meant to be doubtful about himself, but undoubting about the truth; this has been exactly reversed. Nowadays the part of a man that a man does assert is exactly the part he ought not to assert—himself. The part he doubts is exactly the part he ought not to doubt—the Divine Reason."[3]

According to William Willimon, all good preachers ask, "Would Jesus have to be crucified to make this sermon work?"[4] If spiritual direction is delivered without the crucified Christ at the center, then it is only moralistic discourse clothed in religious rhetoric. If Jesus didn't have to die to preach the sermon, the sermon is not *Christian* preaching. As we have said, Jesus related foot-washing to the soul-cleansing power of the atonement. Now, Jesus relates foot-washing to the praxis of discipleship. The challenge to

---

3. Chesterton, *Orthodoxy*, 31.
4. Willimon, "Interview with William Willimon," 41.

wash one another's feet is crucial for the body life of the church and the mission of God. Jesus intended all believers to understand that foot-washing symbolizes both the atonement and the praxis of discipleship. Jesus preached the atonement and the mission of God from his knees and then again at the table.

Upper Room Reflection

How does the convergence of method and message in Jesus' ministry impact our ministry?

Why was Jonathan Edwards concerned about counterfeit humility?

What did Chesterton mean when he said we suffer from humility in the wrong place?

Is your life an object lesson for the gospel?

DAY 21

I Am

"You call me 'Teacher' and 'Lord,' and rightly so, for that is what I am." JOHN 13:13

DIETRICH BONHOEFFER SAID, "ONLY he who believes is obedient, and he who is obedient believes."[1] Good preaching unites doctrine and praxis. When we communicate the gospel we cannot afford to be even one step removed from its practical application. "You call me 'Teacher' and 'Lord,' and rightly so, for that is what I am." At the center of faithful teaching is the "I am" of the gospel. Unless our "I" is wrapped around the "I am" of the one who is faithful and true, our efforts will only bring confusion and distortion.

Christian spirituality aims to submit to Jesus in the first person. We do not sit in the seat of authority, Jesus does. Our aim is to point people to Jesus. Our preaching or teaching or mentoring or parenting should not create a dependency upon ourselves but upon the living Word. If the Lord is not our shepherd—our pastor—then no human pastor will ever make a very good pastor for

---

1. Bonhoeffer, *The Cost of Discipleship*, 69.

us. No pastor will ever become a satisfying substitute for the Lord, no matter how hard he or she tries.

Some people want to experience what it is to follow the Lord Jesus vicariously through their pastor. Instead of living by faith, they want to see their pastor live by faith. They want to look to their pastor for the feeling of reassurance that the Christ life is being lived out. The pastor becomes a symbol for living the life they are either unable or unwilling to live for themselves. Instead of taking up the cross and following Jesus, they want to listen to their pastor talk about the cross. Instead of using their spiritual gifts for God's kingdom work, they want to watch their gifted pastor.

Jesus speaks in the first person six times (John 13:12–17). Each time he underscores the unique way that the disciples are dependent on him. This truth still stands for today's disciples. No one saves us the way Jesus saves us. The work of Christ is unique. No one officiating at the Lord's Supper has shed a drop of blood for our salvation. Only Christ's sacrificial death on the cross redeems us. So when Jesus says, "Do you understand what *I have done for you*?" we know that only he could do for us what we need done.

"My command is this: Love each other as I have loved you. Greater love has no one than this: to lay down one's life for one's friends" (John 15:12–13).

No one else relates to us the way Jesus relates to us. The person of Christ is unique. "You call me 'Teacher' and 'Lord,' and rightly so, for that is what *I am*." There are seven previous "I am" sayings in the Gospel of John, all of them declaring Christ to be the all-sufficient source of our salvation and the ground for our being. The "I am" reality of Jesus is absolutely critical for who we are.

"*I am the bread of life*. Whoever comes to me will never go hungry and whoever believes in me will never be thirsty . . . I am the living bread that came down from heaven. Whoever eats of this bread will live forever. This bread is my flesh, which I will give for the life of the world" (6:35).

"*I am the light of the world*. Whoever follows me will never walk in darkness, but will have the light of life" (John 8:12).

DAY 21

"*I am the gate of the sheep*. . . . I am the gate; whoever enters through me will be saved" (John 10:7, 9).

"*I am the good shepherd*. The good shepherd lays down his life for the sheep. . . . I am the good shepherd; I know my sheep and my sheep know me—just as the Father knows me and I know the Father—and I lay down my life for the sheep" (John 10:11, 14).

"*I am the resurrection and the life*. Anyone who believes in me will live, even though they die; and whoever lives and believes in me will never die" (John 11:25).

"*I am the way and the truth and the life*. No one comes to the Father except through me" (John 14:6).

"*I am the vine; you are the branches*. If you remain in me and I in you, you will bear much fruit; apart from me you can do nothing" (John 15:5).

No one serves us the way Jesus serves us. The humility of Christ is unique. "Now that *I, your Lord and Teacher, have washed your feet*, you also should wash one another's feet" (John 13:14). No one else sets an example the way Jesus does. The example of Christ is unique. "*I have set* you an example that you should do as *I have done* for you" (John 13:15). No one else leads us the way Jesus leads us. The leadership of Christ is unique. "Very truly *I tell you*, servants are not greater than their master, nor are messengers greater than the one who sent them" (John 13:16).

We readily submit to the first-person reality of Christ. Only as Christ saves, serves, exemplifies, explains, and leads can we follow. If Christ goes before, we can follow. Holding fast to the priority of the God-first relationship is the disciple's greatest challenge. To leave the Lord Jesus Christ out of any relationship is to invite disaster. Søren Kierkegaard insisted that God is always "the middle term" in every relationship. No matter how beautiful and blissful a friendship may be, if God is left out, then it is not love "but a mutual and enchanting illusion of love." Real love *always* helps another human being love God and "to be helped by another human being to love God is to be loved."[2]

---

2. Kierkegaard, *Works of Love*, 113.

Upper Room Reflection

The world says, "I am enough" or "That's just the way I am," but the Christian says, "I am who I am by the grace of Christ." How do you experience the difference?

Have you been tempted to live out *your* Christian life vicariously through someone else?

Which of the "I am" sayings do you find especially meaningful?

How can Christ be the center in a friendship with a non-Christian?

DAY 22

Group-Selfishness

"I have set you an example that you should do as I have done for you." JOHN 13:15

JESUS PRACTICED A LOVE that ran contrary to everything the disciples expected. The two disciples on the road to Emmaus summed it up: "We had hoped that he was the one who was going to redeem Israel" (Luke 24:21). Instead, Jesus "made himself and his own as unhappy, humanly speaking, as possible."[1] This is the love that smashes every wishful dream, forcing us to admit that only God can teach us how to love him and every other human being. We have to give up loving people on our terms and love them on God's terms. The way of love conceived by the God who kneels is the most radical kind of love. The world cannot recognize this love, and even many Christians struggle to embrace this love.

The world's idea of love, says Kierkegaard, is "group-selfishness." The world rightly condemns *me-only self-love* as selfish, but when selfishness forms a group of other selfish people the world calls it love. The world demands that selfish people give up a measure of individual selfishness in order to enjoy the privileges of

---

1. Kierkegaard, *Works of Love*, 116.

group-selfishness. This kind of love sacrifices the God relationship and "locks God out or at most takes him along for the sake of appearance."[2] Sanctioned self-love comes in many forms: ethnic compatibility, tribal affinity, denominational loyalty, social familiarity, and generational identity. But to love as Christ loves is to know the difference between "group-selfishness" and being the neighbor Christ calls us to be.

True friendship finds its roots in Christ. We are befriended by Jesus. The old gospel hymn says it well: "What a friend we have in Jesus, all our sins and griefs to bear." Our freedom and capacity to be true friends rests on the fact that we have been befriended by Jesus. The command to love one another in John 13:13 is based on the profoundly deep soul cleansing and healing that only Jesus can do. The love of Christ "sacrifices everything in order to make room for God."[3]

Dietrich Bonhoeffer stated the profound implications of this primary relationship with Christ in his helpful classic *Life Together*. He wrote, "We belong to one another only through and in Jesus Christ."[4] This means that whatever relational neediness we experience issues out of our primary relationship with Jesus Christ. The abide-in-me-first principle of friendship means that all other relationships depend on this one prior and primary relationship. We need others because of Christ and to be in fellowship with Christ means we will be in friendship with others. Every relationship, whether with a Christian or a non-Christian, is centered in our abiding relationship with Christ. As Bonhoeffer says, "a Christian comes to others only through Jesus Christ."[5] This shared experience, within the church, among those who are abiding in Christ, serves as a defense against the selfishness of the human condition.

"The more genuine and the deeper our community becomes, the more will everything else between us recede, the more clearly

---

2. Ibid., 123.
3. Ibid.
4. Bonhoeffer, *Life Together*, 21.
5. Ibid.

and purely will Jesus Christ and his work become the one and only thing that is vital between us. We have one another only through Christ, but through Christ we do have one another, wholly, and for all eternity."[6]

Jesus said, "I have set you an example that you should do as I have done for you" (John 13:15). We ought to be amazed that we can do anything along the lines of Jesus. But by enacting the menial task of foot-washing as his example for loving one another, Jesus chose a task that was both ego deflating and outwardly unimpressive. This bottom-rung, practical necessity was inconsequential, as was the person who typically performed the task. The work required no skill or training to speak of. There are no bragging rights for foot-washers. When Prince William emerged from the hospital carrying a car seat for his newborn son, he did so to the applause and cheers of an adoring crowd of well-wishers. Millions of parents do the same thing daily without applause. That's how it is with foot-washers. The world worries about glass ceilings and room for advancement, but Jesus focused on the basics in the basement. The wisdom of selecting this particular task is that it opens up an infinitude of possibilities. It takes the wind out of the sails of every form of selfishness, even "group-selfishness."

Upper Room Reflection

Why does "group-selfishness" look like love, but isn't love?

How can it be said that all love is sourced in God's love for us?

Why is the love of the God who kneels the most radical kind of love?

How is it that real love opens up an infinitude of possibilities?

---

6. Ibid., 25–26.

DAY 23

Luther's Sermon

"Very truly I tell you, servants are not greater than their master." JOHN 13:16

ONE OF OUR BEST sermons on John 13 comes from the sixteenth-century Reformer Martin Luther, entitled "Sermon for the Thursday Before Easter." Drawing on the example of Jesus, Luther said, "We should be humble, and properly employ the gifts and graces which we have, to the advantage of our brothers and sisters, and that we should despise no one, but rather excuse the shortcomings of our fellow human beings, and help them become better." Luther went on to apply this truth to those who have great responsibility in the church: "Those whom God has endowed with much wisdom and honor, and who are called to the office of the ministry, should be especially intent on practicing zealously this feet-washing, that they may not become guilty of abusing the gifts and authority which they have, but employ them faithfully to the service and welfare of the Church."[1]

Pastor Luther applied Jesus' foot-washing to the home. When parents treated their children kindly and attentively, they fulfilled

---

1. Luther, "Sermon for the Thursday Before Easter," 31.

Christ's example. This humble service translated into bringing children up in the fear of the Lord, ready to do his will. "Husband and wife wash each other's feet if they exercise a forbearing spirit towards each other, avoiding anger and inconsiderate scolding." Luther, in his characteristic way, went further and used the text to address the crisis of corruption in the church.

"I believe that Christ, when he exhibited such humility in washing the feet of His disciples, had in mind the great corruption which, on account of the selfishness and pride of the clergy, would creep into His Church in later years. This great evil began to manifest itself soon after . . ."[2]

Luther objected to reducing Christ's example of humility to a once-a-year liturgical rite. He called it a sham when church leaders made a show of washing the feet of their subordinates. "There is no real humility in these cases," chided Luther, for the bishops are only after their own honor. "They expect still greater homage from the recipients for their condescension." For Luther true foot-washing was not about dirty feet and a show of piety, but about "humbling yourself in such a way as to be ever ready to assist others who have not the gifts which you have." Luther said, "This will demand a precious victory over the old Adam within us, who seeks his own honor and exaltation, and is always more prepared to exercise vengeance and oppression than to do good toward others."[3] The transition from humble service to self-glory occurs when the disciple goes from washing feet to kissing feet. Meeting a need is different from turning an act of humble service into a performance for vain glory. We are not called to condescend to the needy so that we might think more highly of ourselves.

To his credit, Luther saw the highly relational nature of Jesus' example. If we are "to wash one another's feet," Luther insisted we have to be with people. If it means a quickness to bear one another's burdens, Luther said we cannot run off "into deserts and solitudes . . . as formerly the monks did." All leaders, from ancient

2. Ibid., 32.
3. Ibid., 37.

monks to modern pastors, stand to benefit from Luther's practical insight:

> No, it is a Christian duty to wash the feet of others, we must stay where they are. We must be among the people who wade through unclean, filthy places. We must unbend our proud reserve, and though our feet should be clean and pretty, it behooves us to carry water, rags, soap and brush to cleanse and wash the feet of those who need such ablution.[4]

Theological students who aim for an academic career to avoid the messiness of pastoral ministry ought to pay attention to Luther's admonition. True spirituality embraces the body of Christ and the world of our neighbor. A private autonomous spirituality is not an option for any believer. We are all called to sacrifice and service. Are you a people person? I didn't say "people pleaser." In Christ the principle of the cross holds true, "my life for yours." Like our Lord we need to get our hands dirty helping people. All of us need to get in on this work. Our personalities and specialized ministries are no excuse for avoiding people. Whether we are introverts or not, foot-washing, and its *ministry equivalent*, requires all of us to make an effort to relate to people for Christ's sake.

Upper Room Reflection

Who has been patient and nurturing with you?

How does your attitude of people's shortcomings get in the way of you helping them get better?

Why can't we wall off our lives from others?

Can you identify some "ministry equivalents" to foot-washing?

4. Ibid., 38.

DAY 24

Ego Busting

*"Now that you know these things,
you will be blessed if you do them."* JOHN 13:17

AS A COMPASS POINTS to the magnetic north, preaching gets its bearings by pointing to Christ. Jesus concluded this part of his table conversation with a familiar analogy: "Very truly I tell you, servants are not greater than their master, nor are messengers greater than the one who sent them" (John 13:16). Human nature, such as it is, makes Jesus' statement necessary. We wrestle not against flesh and blood, but against inflated egos and an obsession with self-recognition. The devil does more damage through our egos than through any other means. We want to be noticeably superior to even our closest friends and colleagues. Below the surface, the self is in constant agitation for approval and praise and the me monster is always prepared to take action against perceived competitors.

Luke reports that the disciples were arguing "as to which of them was considered to be the greatest" (Luke 22:24). In his account, Jesus compared the disciples to worldly leaders who exerted their egos at the expense of the people, but in John 13, he compares the disciples to himself. In Luke, the bottom line is emphatic: "You are not to be like that." But in John, we get our bearings by comparing ourselves to the Lord Jesus. If we put the two accounts together, we understand both sides of Jesus' message. He offered a negative example (worldly leaders) and a positive example (himself). Both the negative and positive sides of this argument expose a style of leadership that is ingratiating and self-serving. There is a hidden vanity in much of our leadership that deserves to be nullified.

The upper room is an ego-busting experience. Jesus calls into question our striving for self-recognition and honor and negates our vain attempts to create an honorific culture. This text causes us to weigh the difference between encouraging our brothers and sisters and lifting up their egos to make them feel good about themselves. We may need to rethink the institutional strategy that seeks to honor people in order to enhance institutional prestige. Awards and honorary degrees seem out of sync with John 13 and Luke 22. Oppressive forms of leadership are not redeemed by an awards ceremony presided over by a leader who prides himself or herself on being a benefactor (Luke 22:25).

For disciples the comparison is always between ourselves and Christ. If this comparison penetrates our thinking, we will be better off. No disciple ever says, "I am greater than Jesus Christ." But sometimes our actions speak louder than our words. When we object to tasks that we consider beneath us, we ignore the foot-washing humility of Jesus. Keeping the comparison between our Lord and Teacher in the forefront of our inner dialogue and self-talk will help in nurturing true regard for our brothers and sisters in Christ. This will also check our sinful disposition to be more concerned about what people think of us than what they think of Christ. No one ever admits that they are more into self-praise than praising Christ, but the danger is real.

The American way rejects the notion that we have a master of any kind, even the Lord Jesus. The autonomous-individual-entrepreneurial-democratic-therapeutic self is unaware of anyone being king. At its core the Christian life is countercultural, but beware of thinking this tension with culture looks and feels cool.

On this side of eternity we do not rise above the soul-searching humility of the Beatitudes.

Jesus' foot-washing example and his Sermon on the Mount Beatitudes are in perfect harmony. The path to blessing is counterintuitive, running against the current of both conventional and "relevant" thinking. The God who kneels shows us the path to salt and light impact. He reveals the power of visible social righteousness and the secret to the hidden righteousness of true spirituality. Jesus' teaching and actions interface perfectly.

Good preaching and good conversation ends with God's benediction: "Now that you know these things, you will be blessed if you do them." Knowing and doing are held together tightly. In *theory*, the Christian life is nothing, but in *action* it is altogether redemptive and revolutionary. We are saved by faith alone, but saving faith is never alone. Merit-based works' righteousness inevitably leads to legalism and moralism, but the riches of God's mercy invariably inspire the works of righteousness. As Paul said, we work out our salvation with "fear and trembling," because "it is God who works in [us] to will and act according to his good purpose" (Phil 2:12–13).

Upper Room Reflection

How do you cope with the tug-of-war between feelings of inferiority and feelings of superiority?

What have you found helpful in taming the me monster?

What were the negative and positive spiritual directions the disciples received in the upper room?

How is the theory of the Christian life tested in your life?

DAY 25

A Betrayer

"Very truly I tell you, one of you is going to betray me."
JOHN 13:21

JOHN'S NARRATIVE DESCRIPTION OF Jesus' response to Judas is surprisingly matter of fact. On the face of it, John provides a simple narrative of how Jesus interacted with Judas. However, there is more to this text than meets the eye. John 13:18–30 offers a theology of acceptance and rejection, a case study in loyalty and betrayal, that leads the disciple to critical self-examination. As much as we might like to, we cannot put what Judas did out of our minds. The dynamic interplay between Jesus and Judas hits too close to home.

This passage is also important in demonstrating how we are to love our enemies. John's well-crafted narrative captures the essence of Jesus' interaction with Judas and the disciples, and in the process offers a practical example of loving nonresistance. Jesus has literally gotten up from his knees and put on his outer clothing, but figuratively speaking he is still on his knees. In the midst of this deep relational conflict, he demonstrates great humility and shows us what it means to go the extra mile with our enemies.

DAY 25

The authoritative "I" characteristic of Jesus' deliberate speech (John 13:12–17) continues in this next section as well (13:18–21). We count seven first-person references. At the center of good spiritual direction is the authoritative "I am who I am" Christ focus. Jesus succinctly articulates the rationale for true preaching: "I am telling you now . . . so that . . . you will believe that I am who I am" (John 13:19).

Jesus is Lord. Who he is and what he has done is always the gospel's focus. The ambassador of Christ never loses sight of King Jesus. Jesus turns from positive spiritual direction, preaching the Jesus way ("you also should wash one another's feet"—John 13:14) to discerning the troubling reality of rejection and betrayal. Yet, the central focus remains the same: "I am who I am." This must be true of our spiritual direction and preaching as well. No matter how conflicted the situation may be, the fallen human condition and God's redemptive provision in Christ are always in view. Even in the midst of betrayal talk, the focus is redemptive: "so that you will believe that I am who I am" (John 13:19).

His calculated move to inform the disciples of a betrayer in their midst was not designed to protect his reputation but to strengthen their faith. He gave the disciples this heads up so they would not be blindsided. The struggle between belief and unbelief was right there in the upper room. Jesus spoke into that struggle: "I am not referring to all of you; I know those I have chosen" (John 13:18). The providence of God is deeply personal: "I know those I have chosen." The predestinating power of the sovereign Lord of the universe is not dissipated in generic abstractions and categorical generalities but extends to the particular person. True human individuality finds its support in the Creator of humanity, who is not a generic power, but the triune Father, Son and Holy Spirit. This image-of-God individuality is further supported by the singular revelation of the Incarnate One, God enfleshed in a particular human being, who was sent on a mission to save us from our sins. The electing, predestinating, adopting power of God issues from the mind of God and refers directly to the individual in the most personal way possible. "For he chose us in him before the creation of the world to be holy and blameless in his sight" (Eph 1:4). The reality of this personal chosenness does not preclude personal responsibility. We need not question Judas' capacity to act according to his own mind and heart, but even his power to act independently is derived from God.

This gift that God insists on giving to us can be used either for or against God. Author Rob Bell wrote a popular book not long ago entitled *Love Wins*, in which he argues that sooner or later God's mercy wins and everyone gets out of the hell they have chosen. Everyone meets Jesus, whether in this life or the next. Everyone wins in the end. It doesn't matter whether a person is an atheist or an agnostic, a Muslim or a Hindu, the love of God wins in the end and everyone is saved. There is no final judgment and ultimately no wrath of God that needs to be propitiated by the substitutionary death of Christ. Bell asks, "What makes us think that after a lifetime, let alone hundreds or even thousands of years, somebody who has consciously chosen a particular path away from God suddenly wakes up one day and decides to head in the completely opposite direction?"[1] That's the hope. According to Rob Bell salvation is like evolution: given enough time the good life happens. The gates of heaven are always open. Like choosing the ending of a movie, Bell claims we have a choice of stories. There's the bad story in which billions perish in endless torment or a better story where everybody enjoys "God's good world together with no disgrace or shame."[2]

Bell argues that everybody is saved sooner or later, whether in this life or in the futuristic ages to come. Heaven and hell are within you and eventually heaven wins. Bell resolves the dilemma of human destiny not through divine providence, but through the eventual good sense of the existential self to determine the right path in open-ended freedom. Bell replaces the sovereign mind of God with the sovereign self. Instead of resting in the fact that God knows those who are his, and in spite of the Bible's claim that many

---

1. Bell, *Love Wins*, 104.
2. Ibid., 111.

DAY 25

refuse to come to God, Bell gives that power to the individual self—everyone will sooner or later embrace God's love.

Rob Bell's theology expects to see Judas in heaven, but in the Bible, Judas stands as a one-man argument against universalism. He represents the individual who has had every advantage to receive Christ, yet persists in his refusal. Judas insisted on unbelief, and in the end, he preferred to be used by Satan rather than follow Jesus.

Upper Room Reflection

Why is learning to love our enemies a necessary prerequisite for following Jesus?

What do you make of the fact that in God's eyes there is no generic humanity, that everyone is personally and fully known to God?

How do you reconcile Judas-style freedom with the sovereignty of God?

Do you agree that Judas is a one-man argument against universalism?

DAY 26

Psalm 41

"But this is to fulfill the passage of Scripture: 'He who shared my bread has lifted up his heel against me.'" JOHN 13:18

THE GOSPEL NARRATIVE DEMONSTRATES how Jesus processed this internal crisis. From the dialogue an implicit model of spiritual direction emerges that is important for us to emulate. Jesus gained perspective by lining up Psalm 41 with his experience of Judas. Jesus prayed the Psalms daily and these prayers informed his self-understanding. The Psalms provided the emotional grid through which he interpreted life. Psalm 41 gave prophetic insight and providential sanction to an otherwise unpredictable and perverse turn of events.

Psalm 41 is a psalm of deliverance in the face of the harsh realities of human hate. The Lord watches over the weak and delivers them. He protects, preserves, and sustains them. What makes this psalm especially interesting is the distinction made between the hatred of overt enemies and the betrayal of a close friend. Two metaphors are juxtaposed to capture the hostility of a friend: "He who shared my bread has lifted up his heel against me." To break bread together is a metaphor for intimate fellowship. To lift up the

DAY 26

heel against someone is a metaphor for contempt and deep animosity, especially in Middle Eastern culture.

A scene in the old TV series *The West Wing* captures this deep animosity. President Jeb Bartlett, played by Martin Sheen, is alone in the National Cathedral. The funeral service for his administrative assistant, killed by a drunk driver, has just concluded. As the people leave, the president asks to be left alone in the cathedral for a few minutes. In the darkened sanctuary, an angry Bartlett rails against God. He calls him "vindictive," "a feckless thug." He hurls epithets and expletives. Bartlett lights a cigarette and takes a single puff before he drops it to the floor. Defiantly, he grinds the butt with the sole of his shoe. He turns toward the altar and says, "Go to hell." Throughout the series, the president is portrayed as a sincere Roman Catholic, but in this scene, Bartlett captures the spirit of Judas. The writers may have aimed for the despair of Job or the passion of Jeremiah, but what they got was Judas, a one-time friend turned traitor.

When Jesus lifted Judas' heel to wash and dry his feet, we need not wonder what was going through his mind. This line from Psalm 41 filled Jesus' praying imagination: "Even my close friend, someone I trusted, one who shared my bread, has lifted up his heel against me." But along with this thought was the enduring hope of God's sustaining grace: "But may you have mercy on me, Lord; raise me up, that I may repay them. I know that you are pleased with me, for my enemy does not triumph over me" (Ps 41:9–11).

The metaphor of bread is repeated four more times in John's text. When the disciple whom Jesus loved (John's endearing and self-effacing way of identifying himself) asked him to identify the betrayer, Jesus answered, "It is the one to whom I will give this piece of bread when I have dipped it in the dish" (John 13:26). Then, Jesus dipped the bread in the dish and gave it to Judas. The gesture was such a common and positive sign of favor, not hostility, that no one at the time, including John, made the connection. Twice we are told that Judas took the bread. In a few hours, Judas will give Jesus a customary kiss in the garden (Mark 14:45). Both gestures were traditional signs of hospitality. At the table, Jesus used the passing of the bread to preserve Judas's secret, but in the garden, Judas greeted Jesus with a kiss to identify him for the arresting party.

"As soon as Judas took the bread, Satan entered into him" (John 13:27). The implication is that this genuine act of friendship was the decisive moment at which Judas yielded fully to the tempter's agenda. The way in which Jesus exposed his betrayer gave Judas every possible way out. At the table he could have confessed his sin and turned to Jesus for forgiveness. But Judas pushed past the point of repentance and confession. He steeled his will against Jesus' friendship and pursued a course of cold-hearted betrayal and his suicide.

Jesus gained perspective by praying the Psalms and by focusing on a theology of acceptance. The second aspect of Jesus' spiritual resilience is apparent when we focus on John 13:20: "Very truly I tell you, whoever accepts anyone I send accepts me; and whoever accepts me accepts the one who sent me." Embedded in this dialogue is a simple sentence, said with emphasis, that establishes our shared confidence in our relational participation of the kingdom of God. Jesus roots our fellowship with one another in our abiding acceptance of himself. Christ alone is the ground of our fellowship together. But Jesus goes even further. To accept him is to accept the one who sent him. There is an unbreakable relational connection between believing and belonging. To believe is to belong and to belong is to believe. Our friendship with one another is rooted in our acceptance of the triune God.

Deep relationships are built on deep theology. This social networking is of the highest order and rests on the conviction Jesus stated earlier: "No one can come to me unless drawn by the Father who sent me . . ." (John 6:44). Our acceptance of one another is rooted in a theology of mission ("whoever accepts anyone I send accepts me"). We accept one another on God's terms, not on our terms. And to be in fellowship with one another is to be sent by God. Self-acceptance, friendship, and body life are all inseparably linked to our relationship with the triune God ("and whoever accepts me accepts the one who sent me").

DAY 26

Upper Room Reflection

Can you think of a time when you used the Psalms to process a difficult situation?

Why are we tempted to blame God when the evil that God so hates impacts our lives?

In the face of betrayal, are you willing to draw on God's provision for resilience? What is the alternative?

How God centered are your relationships? Is that hard to assess?

DAY 27

Facing Betrayal

"Very truly I tell you, one of you is going to betray me."
JOHN 13:21

TALK OF BETRAYAL CAUGHT the disciples off guard and troubled Jesus. In addition to praying the Psalms and affirming a theology of acceptance, Jesus processed this crisis with a third spiritual discipline: emotional honesty. "After he had said this, Jesus was troubled in spirit and testified, 'Very truly I tell you, one of you is going to betray me'" (John 13:21).

His troubled soul was apparent to the disciples. Jesus loved Judas and his betrayal was painful to endure. When we allow prayer and meditation on Scripture to guide our emotional response to heartbreaking circumstances we will be far better off than giving in to an emotional meltdown. We may be filled with sorrow and prone to tears, but in the midst of our heartbreak we can cling to God's sustaining grace. Emotional honesty does not mean we slam the door on prayer and rant and rave against the very one who promises comfort and peace and endured the cross.

DAY 27

When we are rushed to the ER we want a medical response team to treat our emergency with skill and expertise. We need nurses and doctors to focus on our crisis with a sense of urgency and proficiency. We depend on a calm and capable medical response to our emergency. Similarly, when believers are in a heartbreaking spiritual crisis it doesn't help to shun the means of grace. Instead of closing down, we need the spiritual discipline to turn to God and express our lament. The cultivated habit of praying the Psalms will encourage our faith and strengthen our resolve. Life in the Spirit distinguishes between emotional transparency and a spiritual meltdown.

Why Judas chose to betray Jesus remains a mystery that the Bible does not attempt to solve. Was it about money, politics, or religion? We do not know. Judas objected to Mary's act of devotion when she anointed Jesus' feet with expensive perfume, saying, "Why wasn't this perfume sold and the money given to the poor?" (John 12:5). But we can't tell from Judas's question whether he was concerned for the poor or even critical of Jesus. Ambiguity surrounds his motive for betrayal. Judas could be the precursor to a radical liberation theologian or the first prosperity gospel preacher. We don't know what his main objection to Jesus was. All we know is that Mary's act of devotion appears to have put Judas over the edge. He went directly to the chief priests, asking, "What are you willing to give me if I deliver him over to you?" (Matt 26:15). This makes it look like money was the motive, but Judas may have been hoping to provoke a crisis that would force Jesus to make a political move.

We know that when Jesus was condemned and sentenced to crucifixion, Judas was "seized with remorse and returned the thirty pieces of silver to the chief priests and the elders." His admission of guilt, "I have sinned for I have betrayed innocent blood," fails to acknowledge who he betrayed (Matt 27:3–4).

Betrayal is not limited to one of Jesus' former disciples. We continue to wrestle with the Judas dynamic in our lives and in the church today. A friend for more than twenty years announced that he was leaving his wife and three children for another woman. He admitted that his wife was loving and that his marriage was good, but he insisted that he could go deeper spiritually with this other woman. His delusional claim was shocking and evil. He confused lust with love and infatuation with true spirituality. A cadre of friends, pastors, and counselors tried to reason with him, befriend him, and warn him, but all to no effect. He spiritualized his situation and rationalized his betrayal. He claimed God told him to leave his wife. He was as deceived as Judas was. Meanwhile, his wife by God's grace has shown resilience. She is steadfast in her love for Christ. The pain she suffers is not unlike that of a martyr. In spite of betrayal, she remains faithful. Her Savior knows what it feels like. "I take considerable comfort," she said, "knowing that Jesus knows the pain of betrayal. I don't feel so alone in my pain."

Upper Room Reflection

How does emotional transparency differ from self-pity?

In a spiritual crisis what spiritual disciplines are required?

In the midst of a life-shattering crisis how does the truth of Hebrews 12:2–3 and Romans 8:17–18 impact your life?

How can we strengthen our determination to remain faithful to the end?

DAY 28

Love Your Enemies

"Love your enemies and pray for those who persecute you, that you may be children of your Father in heaven."
MATTHEW 5:44

IT IS SOBERING TO realize that a person can be as close to Jesus as Judas was and yet refuse to believe. No Christian wants to think about Judas, but Martin Luther saw in Judas a warning for all believers, especially the leaders of the church. In his Maundy Thursday sermon, Luther marveled that Judas remained unaffected by "the ceremony of foot-washing and by the solemn words of Christ." Instead of being humbled, Judas "meditated all the while how he could betray his Master and get the thirty pieces of silver." For Luther, Judas was an example of what happens to church leaders who become "so engaged in temporal matters" that they neglect Christ, his word, and their pastoral responsibilities. "Let no one think they are exempt from such temptation. Let us exercise pure humility, imitating Christ who, with towel in hand, arises from the table to wash the feet of others, who thinks not first of himself, but how he may be of service to his brothers and sisters." We must cultivate "a spirit of lowliness, and thrust the devil aside with his prompting to pride and arrogance. If we yield to him and become filled with self-esteem, we are lost; we are then no longer disciples of Jesus, but of Judas."[1]

The most remarkable truth of this passage is how Jesus continued to love Judas in spite of the intentions of his heart. Jesus knew from the beginning that Judas would betray him (John 6:64), but he never identified Judas that way until the end. He maintained his betrayer's cover. His references were always oblique: "The words I have spoken to you—they are full of the Spirit and life. Yet there are some of you who do not believe." When Peter spoke on behalf of the twelve, pledging their loyalty, Jesus replied, "Have I not chosen you, the Twelve? Yet one of you is a devil!" (John 6:70).

Knowing, as he did, the contempt and duplicity that lurked in Judas's heart, and yet to welcome the traitor in table fellowship and to count him among the twelve, can only be said to be the greatest act of long-suffering love. Jesus said, "Learn from me, for I am gentle and humble in heart" (Matt 11:29). With respect to Judas, Jesus shows us what it means to love our enemy. It is one thing to endure opposition from outsiders, to weather their scorn and criticism, but it is much harder to endure the intimate presence of one's suspected enemy. If we reread the Gospel narrative with this fact in mind, we get some inkling as to the constant pressure Jesus was under. Yet Jesus let this situation play out, always giving Judas the full benefit of his fellowship, teaching, and spirituality. Jesus bore this intimate reproach without resentment or bitterness. Judas never became an excuse for anything less than total love. "The wickedness of our neighbor," writes John Chrysostom, "is not strong enough to cast us out of our own virtue."[2]

If we take Jesus' example to heart and embrace the power of the Holy Spirit we will not allow the Judas types to set the agenda and rob us of Christlike gentleness and meekness. What was true of Jesus must be true of his disciples. Jonathan Edwards commends his example this way: "Not one word of bitterness escaped him . . .

---

1. Luther, "Sermon for the Thursday Before Easter," 33, 34, 40.
2. Chrysostom, "Homilies on St. John," 262.

nor was there the least desire for revenge."[3] Thankfully, most of us do not have to contend with a Judas, so it should be easier for us to show love to the obnoxious brother or the difficult sister in Christ. If Jesus could wash the feet of his betrayer, I should be able to be patient with my well-intentioned but misguided brother.

When Jesus informed the disciples that there was a betrayer in their company, he put Judas on notice. However, I doubt that Judas really believed that Jesus knew the intentions of his heart. Judas's unbelief colored his judgment in every way. He was living in the dark and he must have projected that mind-set onto others, including Jesus. His denial of Jesus' wisdom affected how he received this warning. He had grown accustomed to hearing but not really listening to Jesus. He was one of the twelve. He was at the center of the ministry, but he had been living in denial for a long time. What attracted him to Jesus in the first place we do not know. We see this pattern of attraction without discipleship in the church today. Judas was part of a movement bigger than himself. In his mind, he stood above the crowd, and as the movement's CFO he was entrusted with an enviable task. But he didn't know Jesus. The Master's teaching was only background music to the movement's projected growth. For Judas the Sermon on the Mount was religious rhetoric—part of the public relations campaign. Even though his judgment was clouded, Judas must have been surprised that Jesus suspected him.

Loving discernment is neither naive nor cynical (Phil 1:9–11). Love sees what there is to see, but always in a way that is consistent with our identity in Christ. Jesus could afford to be patient with Judas because "he had come from God and was returning to God" (John 13:3). When our identity and our eternity are secure, we can allow ourselves to love our enemies and pray for our persecutors. We can hold our ground, turn the other cheek, and under duress we can walk the second mile (Matt 5:39, 44). We can even break bread with the enemy.

---

3. Edwards, *Charity and Its Fruits*, 84.

Upper Room Reflection

How is confronting our enemy different from enabling or condemning him?

Disciples should be as wise as serpents and as harmless as doves. How does this apply to loving our enemy?

Has an enemy ever become an excuse for your disobedience?

How is your love for those who threaten you a sign of your security in Christ?

DAY 29

Self-Examination

"His disciples stared at one another, at a loss to know which of them he meant." JOHN 13:22

JESUS' REFUSAL TO NAME Judas explicitly had the effect of unsettling the other eleven disciples. "His disciples stared at one another, at a loss to know which of them he meant" (John 13:22). The disciples had been arguing over who among them was the greatest (Luke 22:24). Now they were looking at one another with suspicion and doubt, wondering who was the traitor. Jesus was responsible for this sudden change in focus. He gave the benediction and turned the conversation to the subject of betrayal. The group dynamic shifted from the positive to the negative in a sentence.

For those who run an organization and who feel it is their duty to keep morale up this doesn't seem like the most responsible thing to do. Why not pull Judas aside privately and confront him with your suspicions (Matt 18:15)? Or, if you are going to raise the matter in the group, at least name the betrayer directly so a cloud of suspicion doesn't hang over the whole group. Jesus' strategy prompts us to ask, was this the loving thing to do? Why jeopardize the disciples' peace of mind for the sake of Judas's anonymity?

We have already seen from the text that the purpose of the conversation was to strengthen the disciples' faith in Christ (John 13:19). Jesus' loving discernment drew a line between preparing the disciples for betrayal and naming the betrayer. If Jesus had explicitly named Judas, a sword-wielding Peter may have taken matters into his own hands the way he did in the garden of Gethsemane (John 18:10). Ironically, by preserving Judas's anonymity, Jesus protected Judas from harm. His loving nonresistance allowed evil to run its course. Whatever consternation the disciples felt was a necessary emotion for participating with Jesus in this concrete demonstration of long-suffering love. The disciples were not asked if they were willing to participate, but by virtue of following Jesus they were subject to the necessity of patient endurance. Discipleship has an emotional impact. To abide in Christ is to follow his path and bear the cross. This cannot be done without an emotional toll. These upper room relational dynamics will continue to be experienced by all those who follow the Lord Jesus.

Another reason for Jesus to involve the disciples in this emotional dilemma was to alert them to the imminent danger of betrayal and denial. Personal self-examination was more important than singling out the betrayer. It was better for the disciples to feel their vulnerability than to pounce on Judas. The prophet reminds us that "the heart is deceitful and desperately wicked" (Jer 17:9). "So, if you think you are standing firm, be careful that you don't fall!" (1 Cor 10:12). Judas's actions were premeditated and malicious, but in a few hours all the disciples would succumb to fear and flee from Jesus in his hour of crisis. As uncomfortable as this scene may be, Jesus orchestrated this soul-searching moment. It is wise for us to examine our loyalty to Jesus. The very idea of Judas ought to make us nervous.

Upper Room Reflection

If you had been in the upper room, how would you have reacted to Jesus' warning?

DAY 29

Why did Jesus put the whole group on notice?

Jesus used the *act* of betrayal rather than *Judas himself* as grounds for self-examination. What is the difference?

How does God orchestrate self-examination in your life?

DAY 30

Self-Betrayal

"If we claim to have fellowship with him and yet walk in the darkness, we lie and do not live out the truth." 1 JOHN 1:6

JUDAS BETRAYED NOT ONLY Jesus, but himself. He proved to be his own worst enemy, refusing to heed Jesus' gentle prejudgment warning that might have saved him. Judas had every advantage. He had been with Jesus from the beginning. He witnessed the miracles and listened to the Master's preaching. He was one of the twelve. He experienced firsthand the intimacy of table fellowship and the public impact of feeding the multitudes. He observed transformed lives and experienced the mounting tension with the religious authorities. He walked with Jesus from Galilee to Judah. He ate, slept, and prayed with Jesus. When many disciples left because Jesus' teaching was offensive, Judas remained. He was isolated and alone in the company of Jesus and his disciples. And in the end Jesus washed his feet.

DAY 30

JOHN CHRYSOSTOM, ONE OF the greatest prophet-pastors in the early church, died in 407, but not before issuing a powerful challenge to the followers of the Lord Jesus. John was banished to a remote mountainous town in Armenia, far from his church in Constantinople, because his preaching had offended the emperor. Everything was taken from him—health, church, friends, ministry, and preaching. Everything, but the one thing necessary—the truth that this exhausted fifty-six-year-old prophet-pastor clung to—his devotion to Christ. His letters from exile are strong, uncompromising epistles, written by a resilient saint who steeled himself against the world, the flesh, and the devil. His controlling thought was simple: nothing can destroy you but yourself. Your own worst enemy is not the devil or disease, but your sinful self. Your greatest danger is self-betrayal. Your greatest weakness, littleness of soul.[1]

Chrysostom contended that "no one who is wronged is wronged by another, but experiences this injury at his or her own hands."[2] Nothing that is not self-inflicted can ruin our virtue or destroy our soul. John argued that poverty cannot impoverish the soul. Malignancy cannot malign the character. The lack of health care cannot destroy a healthy soul. Famine cannot famish one who hungers and thirsts for righteousness. No! Not even the devil and death can destroy those who live sober and vigilant lives. Educator Parker Palmer offers a similar insight when he writes, "No punishment anyone lays on you could possibly be worse than the punishment you lay on yourself by conspiring in your own diminishment."[3]

Theologian Jerry Sittser describes the challenge we face this way:

> The difference between despair and hope, bitterness and forgiveness, hatred and love, and stagnation and vitality lies in the decisions we make about what to do in the face of regrets over an unchanging and painful past. We

---

1. Chrysostom, "To Prove That No One," 274.
2. Ibid., 272.
3. Palmer, *The Courage to Teach*, 171.

cannot change the situation, but we can allow the situation to change us. We exacerbate our suffering needlessly when we allow one loss to lead to another. That causes gradual destruction of the soul.... The death that comes through loss of spouse, children, parents, health, job, marriage, childhood, or any other kind is not the worst kind of death there is. Worse still is the death of the spirit, the death that comes through guilt, regret, bitterness, hatred, immorality, and despair. The first kind of death happens to us; the second kind of death happens in us. It is a death we bring upon ourselves if we refuse to be transformed by the first death."[4]

Self-betrayal is the danger, littleness of soul the problem. "Those who do not injure themselves become stronger," wrote Chrysostom, "even if they receive innumerable blows; but they who betray themselves, even if there is no one to harass them, fall of themselves, and collapse and perish."[5] Judas had no one to blame but himself. When he left the upper room, he walked out into the night, not only literally, but figuratively. Judas chose the darkness over the light, even though he had been surrounded by the light of Christ for three years. Years later, the Apostle John implied in his epistle that Judas's experience was not uncommon. Professing believers like Judas experience everything that Christ and the church have to offer, but in the end, they are not one of the disciples and the truth comes out.

My fear is that Judas was in person what our culture is en masse. T. S. Eliot in *Thoughts after Lambeth* captures the ethos of Judas writ large over the canvas of culture when he writes, "The World is trying the experiment of attempting to form a civilized but non-Christian mentality. The experiment will fail; but we must be very patient in awaiting its collapse; meanwhile redeeming the time: so that the Faith may be preserved alive through the dark

---

4. Sittser, *A Grace Disguised*, 86–87.
5. Chrysostom, "To Prove That No One," 280.

DAY 30

ages before us; to renew and rebuild civilization, and save the World from suicide."[6]

Upper Room Reflection

Why was Judas without excuse?

How do we resist the temptation of hiding our true thoughts and feelings in plain view of our brothers and sisters in Christ?

Why is the betrayal of Jesus a form of self-betrayal?

Are there practical ways we can resist self-betrayal and littleness of soul?

---

6. Quoted in Webster, "Modern Mandrake," 11.

DAY 31

Treachery

"As soon as Judas took the bread, Satan entered into him."
JOHN 13:27

JUDAS' FEIGNED INNOCENCE, "SURELY not I, Rabbi?" thinly concealed a heart that had grown hard and resistant to Jesus. Judas hated Jesus and Jesus knew it. The verdict against Judas had already been delivered by Jesus: "Woe to the man who betrays the Son of Man! It would be better for him if he had not been born" (Matt 26:23–25). After the betrayal, we are told by Matthew that Judas was "seized with remorse." He tried to return the thirty pieces of silver. "I have sinned," he announced, "for I have betrayed innocent blood." The chief priests and elders replied, "What is that to us? That's your responsibility" (Matt 27:4).

In the end Judas came to the realization that he had wronged an innocent man. According to the Apostle Peter, Judas's remorse stopped short of repentance. His despair does not appear to have led to deliverance. The finality of suicide sealed Judas's tragic and willful determination. In the book of Acts, it is Peter who brings closure to the Judas saga. He quotes from the Psalms to describe Judas's fate: "May his place be deserted; let there be no one to dwell in it" (Ps 69:25; see Acts 1:20). The disciples found it fitting that Judas should be memorialized by a cemetery known as the Field of Blood.

The Apostle John's take on Judas may be expressed in his letter, when he wrote:

> Dear children, this is the last hour and as you have heard that the antichrist is coming, even now many antichrists have come. This is how we know it is the last hour. They went out from us, but they did not really belong to us. For if they had belonged to us, they would have remained with us; but their going showed that none of them belonged to us (1 John 2:18–19).

John's definition of the antichrist is this: "Whoever denies that Jesus is the Messiah. Such a person is the antichrist—denying the Father and the Son" (1 John 2:22). This spirit of the antichrist can be found wherever the incarnation of Jesus is denied. John warns the believers that this spirit of denial and deception is "already in the world" (1 John 4:3; 2 John 7). The same power that was at work in Judas is still at work in the world and remains a threat to the church. Without this clear-sighted spiritual diagnosis believers are in danger of becoming confused and disillusioned, not unlike Judas.

Not long ago I was invited along with other pastors to the home of a church leader who wanted us to meet his gay partner. I went with the expectation of having a good conversation. I wanted to understand how this gay couple related their sexuality to their faith in Christ. Sitting across from the church leader's gay partner, and after an interesting conversation on his expertise in software, I asked, "How do the two of you discuss theology?" He looked at me, like he didn't understand the question. So, I repeated it, saying, "You know, how do you talk about the Christian faith?" He answered, "Oh, we never talk about the faith. I'm not a Christian. I'm not a believer." The clear, if not casual, confession of unbelief fit with the irreconcilable nature of the Christian faith and homosexual practice. To deny that Jesus is the Christ was really no big deal for the gay partner of a church leader, nor did intimate sexual relations with an unbeliever seem to bother the church leader.

Listening to the narrative exchange between Jesus and Judas causes us to examine our own reactions to Jesus. Far from bringing out the best, Jesus' upper room humility brought out the worst in Judas. Jesus' words and actions were the last straw for Judas. He wanted a messiah who met his expectations and Jesus disappointed him deeply. It is dangerous to accept Jesus on our terms because a fantasy faith will fail every time. With malice in his heart Judas turned away from Jesus in disgust. Satan was pleased.

Judas is gone. He might have slammed the door on the way out. Most likely he was angry enough, but I doubt that he did anything to give himself away. The other disciples thought he was sent on a mission to buy whatever was needed for the Passover or to give something to the poor (John 13:29). There was still time for Judas to reconsider and repent, but he was determined. He went out into the night. He was set to betray the Master, himself, and everything he stood for. Judas's dark night of the soul was utterly unredemptive.

Upper Room Reflection

What makes Judas's unbelief especially dangerous?

Did John's definition of the antichrist include Judas?

Is it possible for professing believers to be practicing unbelievers?

What is the danger of confusing remorse with repentance?

DAY 32

Humble Glory

"Now is the Son of Man glorified and God is glorified in him." JOHN 13:31

THE WHOLE PASSION NARRATIVE is about the glory of God, from foot-washing to the cross. The upper room may seem like an unlikely place to bring up glory, but this heavenly theme has been on Jesus' mind throughout the ordeal. Earlier in the week, when he predicted his death, he said,

> "The hour has come for the Son of Man to be glorified. Very truly I tell you, unless a kernel of wheat falls to the ground and dies, it remains only a single seed. . . . Now, my soul is troubled, and what shall I say? 'Father, save me from this hour'? No, it was for this reason I came to this hour. Father, glorify your name!" (John 12:23–27).

These words invoke an immediate response from heaven. A voice declares, "I have glorified it, and will glorify it again" (John 12:28). To the crowd the voice sounded like thunder, but to Jesus it was the Father's confirmation. Between the Father and the Son there is no separation other than that which will be assumed on the cross—our sin. The Father, Son, and Holy Spirit are together in this mission.

With Judas gone, Jesus speaks of glory. The beginning of the end has been set in motion and true to form Jesus understands this critical turning point theologically. "Now is the Son of Man glorified and God is glorified in him. If God is glorified in him, God will glorify the Son in himself, and will glorify him at once" (John 13:31–32). There is no lingering battle in Jesus' mind over Judas. Judas is gone and Jesus moves on. Remorse and resentment are not allowed to control what comes next. May Christ's example embolden us to move on when we have been betrayed. Jesus doesn't even allow Judas to ruin the evening. His bold statement, "Now is the Son of Man glorified . . ." is another "get behind me Satan" moment. The devil's machinations are no match for the divine momentum of grace that triumphs over sin and death.

This declaration underscores the mutuality and immediacy of God's glory. Father, Son, and Holy Spirit are working together as one. It is this divine partnership, this harmony of purpose, mission, and accomplishment that is truly glorious. A theology of the cross and a theology of glory are inseparable. There is no glory apart from the cross and no cross apart from God's glory. John says as much in his prologue: "We have seen his glory, the glory of the one and only Son, who came from the Father, full of grace and truth" (John 1:14).

"Full of grace and truth" is the best way to capture the glory of God in Christ. This glory extends from the upper room, when Jesus was on his knees washing the disciples' feet, to heaven's throne, when every knee shall bow and every tongue confess that Jesus Christ is Lord. His glory was manifest when he was laid in a manger and when he was seated at the right hand of God the Father. The glory of God is manifest whenever and wherever the will of God is realized. Paradoxically, Judas' departure from the upper room triggered in Jesus' praying imagination the very real sensation of being in the center of the Father's will.

The glory of God is what obedience feels like, even when it lands you in the middle of a difficult situation. God's glory is

DAY 32

far from being incompatible with suffering and tribulation. On the contrary, the glory of God often shines brightest in times of greatest pain and anguish. This glory is found in the humility that ranges from foot-washing to the cross, because in the midst of this passion, God looks upon the disciple with favor. The Aaronic benediction captures the meaning of God's glory: "The Lord bless you and keep you; the Lord make his face shine on you and be gracious to you; the Lord turn his face toward you and give you peace" (Num 6:24–26).

In some theologies, the glory of God comes only at the end. God's glory is found in the realized eschatology of our new, glorified, and resurrected bodies and in the final judgment. This division between a theology of the cross and a theology of glory came about as a reaction to ecclesial triumphalism, when "the glory of God" became an excuse for lavish displays of material wealth and grand cathedrals. Luther defended the theology of the cross against a church enraptured by worldly power and glory. A modern variation on this abuse of God's glory is evident in a prosperity gospel that claims that Jesus died on the cross so that Christians can realize their dreams of financial success. When the glory of God is co-opted by visions of worldly power and personal success it is yanked from its biblical roots and severed from its tie to the humility of the cross.

Jesus spoke too much of glory in the midst of suffering for us to ignore God's glory's deep roots in humility. His words capture the immediacy of God's glory: "Now" is the Son glorified. The glory of God is not reserved for the future, but is experienced in the present as an immediate sign of God's favor. And then we read that the Son will be glorified "at once." This is the glory associated with humility and obedience. God's glory shines in the crowning of the King of kings *and* in the cross of Christ. The immediacy of God's favor and the blessing of God's glory in the midst of a life marked by the cross is the new way to follow Jesus. The God who kneels inspires a fresh look at the glory of God.

Upper Room Reflection

When you are dealt a blow are you able to bounce back and stay focused?

Why is the power of resentment so destructive in the life of a follower of Jesus?

How is the prosperity gospel a distortion of the glory of God?

How does God's glory rooted in humility impact discipleship?

DAY 33

A False Literal

"Where I am going, you cannot come." JOHN 13:33

RENEWED BY THIS GLORY, Jesus has the personal security and steadfast confidence to turn his attention to the disciples. He prepares them for what is about to take place. He addresses them as "my children," a term of endearment. He underscores their abiding relationship. He reassures them of his love. Jesus is off his knees, fully dressed and seated at the table, but the humility of the God who kneels prevails. Jesus seeks to comfort and encourage his disciples:

> "My children, I will be with you only a little longer. You will look for me, and just as I told the Jews, so I tell you now: Where I am going, you cannot come" (John 13:33).

At first glance this applies only to the original group of disciples who were literally with Jesus. He was concerned to prepare them for his physical departure and to guide them into a new phase of discipleship. They could no longer walk with Jesus nor enjoy table fellowship. They could not see him heal the sick or hear him preach. He was no longer there for them in a literal sense and they had to adjust. The New Testament is a testimony to the fact that the disciples made this adjustment amazingly well. Of course, they did so not in their own strength, but through the power and wisdom of the Spirit of the risen and ascended Lord.

In the upper room, Peter found Jesus' statement especially difficult to grasp. Like a patient in a doctor's office being informed of a difficult diagnosis, Peter missed what Jesus had to say about the new commandment. He was still focused on the line, "Where I am going, you cannot come." He seems to speak on behalf of the group, voicing their shared concern, when he says, "Lord, where are you going?" (John 13:36).

The absence of a literal, physical Jesus is as relevant for us as it was for the original band of disciples. The disciples had to learn how to follow Jesus without his physical presence. This is true for today's disciples as well. The danger of a "false literal" confronts the church today as it always has. Given the absence of Jesus, we are given to substitutes that stand in the place of a physical Jesus.

The literal concreteness of a pre-Easter Jesus becomes transposed into the false literal experience of spiritual leaders who focus attention on themselves. It can be powerful personalities, but it can also be ecclesiastical bureaucracies, church buildings, cherished practices, and spiritual experiences that stand in the place of Jesus. Traditional religious rituals, megachurch superstars, and down-home country pastors can substitute for the Spirit of the risen Christ. Instead of the church dependent on the fruit and gifts of the Spirit of Christ we give ourselves to "Christian" idols that stand in the place of a literal Jesus. Instead of shared leadership and every-member ministry, believers tragically live out their faith vicariously through charismatic pastors who they can see and touch. Jesus is gone, but he has not left a vacuum. The gift of the Holy Spirit makes possible the real presence of the risen and exalted Christ in the body of Christ, the church.

I recently attended an installation service for one my students. He became the new senior pastor in a large congregation. My friend is a humble, solid believer. He is a mature pastor, a gifted preacher and leader, grounded in the word of God and committed to the priesthood of all believers. But if the service was any indication my friend will have an uphill battle, because many in his congregation expect him to be their new Moses. People want their pastor to be a substitute for Jesus. They want the "first family" of the church to be everything their families are not, but hope they can become. They want a pastor who will come down from Mount Sinai each week and deliver the word of God. It's his job to lead them to the promised land. They fixate on their little messiah in place of the real Messiah. In the installation service for my pastor friend the congregation applauded when one of the speakers applied Isaiah's messianic prophecy to their new pastor, "For unto us a son is given . . . and the government will rest on his shoulders" (Isa 9:6). I left amazed at the pressure my friend was under to meet his congregation's expectations.

These two paragraphs on the immediacy of God's glory (John 13:31–32) and Jesus' literal departure (John 13:33) are related in a significant way. The individuals who confuse worldly glory with God's humble glory invariably coalesce around charismatic personalities and powerful organizations to give their spiritual experience concrete meaning and inspiration. This false literal serves as a substitute for fixing our eyes on Jesus the author and finisher of our faith (Heb 12:2). These stand-ins for Christ's real presence in the body of Christ cause many to miss out on what it means to follow Jesus. The temptation is strong to substitute a false glory for the humble glory of the cross.

Upper Room Reflection

What is the temptation of the false literal?

Have you ever made someone or something into a substitute for Jesus?

How do our expectations distort the meaning of discipleship?

Who defines what it means to glorify God and enjoy him forever?

DAY 34

A New Way to Follow

*"Love one another. As I have loved you,
so you must love one another."* JOHN 13:34

JESUS LAYS OUT A new commandment. This is how the followers of Jesus are to live in the in-between time, between "the already" and the "not yet." The Apostle John wrote in his epistle, "No one has ever seen God; but if we love one another, God lives in us and his love is made complete in us" (1 John 4:12). The invisible God's visibility is revealed today in and through the body of believers marked by the love of Christ. John defined the meaning of this love. "This is love: not that we loved God, but that he loved us and sent his Son as an atoning sacrifice for our sins. Dear friends, since God so loved us, we also ought to love one another" (1 John 4:10). Once again we see the inseparable relationship between the divine atonement and the praxis of discipleship.

In the prologue to his Gospel, John defined the unique and humble visibility of the revelation of God: "No one has ever seen God, but the one and only Son, who is himself God and is in closest relationship with the Father, has made him known" (John

DAY 34

1:18). Salvation history is fulfilled in the one who "being in very nature God . . . made himself nothing" (Phil 2:6–7). The invisible visibility of the hidden God made known in Jesus offers the most profound rationale for today's discipleship. From the beginning and throughout salvation history everything was carefully orchestrated by God to prepare for the stark simplicity of Jesus laid in a manger and nailed to the cross. This is the unadorned sacrifice that saves us from our sin and redeems us for the very presence of God. In the life, death, resurrection, and ascension of Jesus, God remained true to the principle and pattern of the unadorned altar (Exod 20:22–26). The concrete reality of his presence, "full of grace and truth," revealed a glory unlike the world had never seen. For his humble glory revealed his love.

What is new in this new commandment is that love is based on and empowered by the atoning sacrifice of Christ. People have always loved one another. There is love between husbands and wives, parents and children. There is love between friends. In carnal affection, even adulterers and adulteresses love one another, and criminals can be said to love one another. But this new commandment calls us to love the way Christ loves. This love is not based on commonsense self-interest but on costly grace and the principle of the cross ("my life for yours"). New commandment love is consistent with the new covenant and the Great Commission. This heart-scripted love communicates to the world that we belong to the Lord Jesus. "By this everyone will know that you are my disciples, if you love another" (John 13:35). New commandment love makes concrete and real Jesus' agenda laid out in the Sermon on the Mount. The false literal, a stand-in for the real presence of Christ, is not allowed to substitute for the real demonstration of Christ's love.

Peter's reaction to all of this is typical of our own. Like Peter, we insist on our own version of heroic spirituality. We have in mind how we are going to make a name for ourselves in Christian service. Peter boldly claimed, "I will lay down my life for you" (John 13:37). His boast is reminiscent of Jesus' temptation in the wilderness, when the devil led him to Jerusalem and had him stand on the highest point of the temple. "If you are the Son of God," Satan said, "throw yourself down from here" (Luke 4:9). We are tempted to do something spectacular to prove ourselves, to rise above the average, ordinary Christian and distinguish ourselves in some special way.

In the moment, Peter had his own visions of grandeur. His dream of self-sacrifice eclipsed the reality of Christ's sacrifice. The subtle danger of spiritual narcissism is unnerving because it is so easy to spot in others and so terribly difficult to see in ourselves. We are prone to false dreams of courage and conviction that vanish when we awaken to the harsh realities of costly discipleship. We nurture the need for approval and commendation in a self-preoccupied culture, while Christ is calling us to humble foot-washing. We look up to a spiritual CEO of a huge religious mall, dubiously called a church, but Christ calls us to serve a household of faith in diligence and humility. We want a bold, audacious project that demands heroic sacrifice, yet Christ calls us to care for an invalid parent or teach a fifth-grade Sunday school class.

Upper Room Reflection

How is the invisible God made visible today?

What is the difference between being self-conscious and being self-aware?

What makes the new commandment new?

What has made the Christian life easier or harder than you expected?

DAY 35

Heroic Spirituality

"Lord, why can't I follow you now? I will lay down my life for you." JOHN 13:37

PETER IS RIGHT, OF course. He will end up laying his life down for Christ, but he will do so on God's terms, not his own. By the Sea of Galilee, the risen Lord Jesus said to Peter, "Feed my sheep. Very truly I tell you, when you were younger you dressed yourself and went where you wanted; but when you are old you will stretch out your hands, and someone else will dress you and lead you where you do not want to go" (John 21:18). Oswald Chambers drew this application: "I must never choose the scene of my own martyrdom, nor must I choose the things God will use in order to make me broken bread and poured out wine. . . . Determination and devotion, protestations and vows are born of self-consciousness, and must die out of a disciple."[1]

We follow Jesus on his terms and in his way, not our own. We never graduate from Jesus' Sermon on the Mount Beatitudes. And why would we want to? All eight Beatitudes, from "Blessed

---

1. Chambers, *So Send I You*, 19, 69.

are the poor in spirit" to "Blessed are those who are persecuted," apply to us. John the Baptist's famous line, "He must increase, but I must decrease," is our line, too (John 3:30). Like the Apostle Paul we "work out [our] salvation with fear and trembling, for it is God who works in [us] to will and act according to his good purpose" (Phil 2:12-13). The God who kneels washed our feet and commands us to wash one another's feet.

Jesus worked against the grain of the fallen human condition. He called Peter on his heroic boast. "Will you really lay down your life for me?" Jesus asked. And then, without waiting for a reply, Jesus added, "Very truly I tell you, before the rooster crows, you will disown me three times!" (John 13:38). The early church turned the crowing rooster, a symbol of Peter's denial and repentance, into an icon for watchfulness and vigilance. Early paintings of the Apostle Peter show him holding the keys of heaven with a rooster pictured nearby to remind us of his denial. But the rooster does more than recall Peter's denial, it causes us to think of our own susceptibility to pride, our fear of standing up for Christ, and our vulnerability to denying Christ.

This last extended conversation between Jesus and his disciples before the cross lacked nothing. It had the character of full disclosure and intimate friendship. Jesus left nothing unsaid that should have been said. He washed their feet, filled their minds, shaped their hearts, and transformed the Passover into the Last Supper. He spoke words of comfort: "Do not let your hearts be troubled. Trust in God; trust also in me" (John 14:1); "Peace I leave with you; my peace I give you. I do not give to you as the world gives" (John 14:27). He challenged disciples everywhere when he said, "A time is coming when anyone who kills you will think he is offering a service to God" (John 16:2). Jesus promised them the Holy Spirit and he prayed for them: "My prayer is not that you take them out of the world but that you protect them from the evil one. They are not of the world, even as I am not of it. Sanctify them by the truth; your word is truth" (John 17:15-16).

Everything Jesus said that night in the upper room prepared the disciples for what was coming. The future involved betrayal, denial, persecution, and death, but Jesus in the upper room revealed so much more. He offered his abiding fellowship: "I am the vine; you are the branches . . ." (John 15:5). He promised the comfort and counsel of the Holy Spirit. He spoke of a deepening experience of the glory of God. Jesus prayed, "Father, I want those you have given me to be with me where I am, and to see my glory, the glory you have given me because you loved me before the creation of the world" (John 17:24).

The emotional range in the upper room swung from "I tell you the truth, one of you is going to betray me" (John 13:21) to "I have called you friends, for everything that I learned from my Father I have made known to you" (John 15:15). Jesus was confident, encouraging, and bold: "I have told you these things, so that in me you may have peace. In the world you will have trouble. But take heart! I have overcome the world" (John 16:33). But his tone was also ominous and sad. Jesus warned the disciples that they would "all fall away on account" of him (Matt 26:31). He quoted from the Prophet Zechariah: "I will strike the shepherd, and the sheep of the flock will be scattered" (Zech 13:7; Matt 26:31). Yet the sober realization that he was about to be betrayed by Judas, denied by Peter, and abandoned by the rest of the disciples did not distract Jesus from preparing and praying for all the disciples, including us. There is no place for heroic spirituality either inside or outside the upper room.

Upper Room Reflection

Why do our dreams of Christian service often clash with God's will?

How do we know we are following Jesus in the Jesus way?

What does falling away on Jesus' account look like in your culture?

Are you more fearful of personal humiliation than you are of disappointing your Savior?

DAY 36

An Ego Challenge

"Even if all fall away on account of you, I never will."
MATTHEW 26:33

THE DIFFERENCE BETWEEN JUDAS and Peter is the difference between deception and weakness. Treachery is not the same as timidity. Contempt for Jesus is not the same as false confidence in one's ability to stand for Jesus. Both lead to sin, but being hateful is different from being hurtful. Judas wanted to expose Jesus as a fraud, but Peter wanted to be faithful to Jesus. Judas was filled with regret, but Peter was filled with repentance. We are meant to see ourselves in Peter, but no one was ever meant to identify with Judas.

A crowing rooster should remind us not only of Peter's denials, but of how much we are like Peter. As one writer said, "All disciples can profit by a careful study of how the 'Rock' turned to 'sand' in his most critical test."[1] Peter makes me nervous. Comparing myself to him is like standing too close to the edge of Niagara Falls. Peter's ego drove him to the edge and he fell. If the

---

1. Gill, *Peter the Rock*, 111.

DAY 36

representative disciple, a member of Jesus' inner circle, could fall like that, so can I. The nature of Peter's experience is too close to our own to be ignored. His vulnerability to sin reminds us of our own. We find it easy, all too easy, to identify with him. We share his pride, practice his brand of foolishness, and experience his lack of courage and faithfulness.

Peter's pride was embarrassingly transparent. Not to himself of course, but to all of us who hear him brag. He illustrates the proverb "Pride goes before destruction, a haughty spirit before a fall" (Prov 16:18). When Jesus said, "This very night you will all fall away on account of me," Peter replied, "Even if all fall away on account of you, I never will" (Matt 26:33). It is this bold and brash claim made by the impetuous, outspoken Peter that gets our attention. There is nothing humble about the rhetoric of self-confidence. Peter's chest-thumping one-upmanship is like the pregame hype before the big game. We instinctively ask, "How could Peter say such a thing?" With the rest of the disciples standing right there, Peter's single comment turned loyalty to Jesus into a competition with himself as the self-proclaimed winner (see Gal 6:4). Pride is insidious because it often separates us from reality and from others without us knowing it.

What do you think would have happened if John had pulled Peter aside and said, "Will you get a grip? Listen to yourself! Where do you get off claiming to be better than the rest of us?" We don't read that John or any of the other disciples said anything to Peter. The reason we are seldom confronted about our pride is because pride, although so obvious to others, is such a tough sin to expose to the proud. Pride is a form of self-deception and when we deceive ourselves it is almost impossible for us to see the truth. Like Peter, we believe our own self-talk. What Peter felt was courage and loyalty for the Master was really only self-centered pride! What sounded so bold and spiritual quickly turned into denials and curses. When prides runs its course, it leaves us as it left Peter, disillusioned and frustrated.

Peter's courage depended upon an ego challenge rather than a spiritual challenge. I believe that under certain conditions Peter would have made good on his claim to lay down his life for Jesus (John 13:37). The evidence for this can be seen in the garden of Gethsemane. When Peter was confronted, he reacted by fighting back. As you might expect, if only two disciples were armed, one of them would have had to be Peter (Luke 22:38). Peter drew his sword and cut off the ear of the high priest's servant. Immediately, Jesus commanded Peter, "Put your sword away! Shall I not drink the cup the Father has given me?" (John 18:11). Why was Peter willing to risk his life in hand-to-hand combat in the garden, but afraid to admit to a servant girl that he knew Jesus? This doesn't appear to make sense until one realizes the nature of the conflicting challenges.

In the garden it was a challenge to Peter's bravery, his willingness to fight and his readiness to put his life on the line for the cause. Peter was up to the ego challenge. But alone in the high priest's courtyard, with no surrounding audience, Peter was unwilling to admit that he was one of Jesus' disciples. He was all set to man up for the ego challenge, but he shriveled up when it came to the witness challenge. When his own ego was not in question and his macho image was not threatened, Peter found it easy to deny that he ever knew Jesus. The servant girl got from Peter what an armed centurion would have been unable to extract—a denial! She made it easy for him: "You aren't one of this man's disciples too, are you?" (John 18:17). It is not too difficult to imagine Peter writing this servant girl off as inconsequential. She didn't matter. She didn't deserve the truth. Some people might chalk this up to a low-rung denial, made necessary by the climb up the corporate ladder of success. Does a two-word deflection, "Not me," constitute a denial? Note that Peter was not asked if he believed in Jesus. He was asked if he was "one of his disciples." Dale Bruner writes, "We may not think that we are denying or disowning Christ when we deny or disassociate ourselves from his always problematic Church, but Peter's experience teaches us to think again."[2]

---

2. Bruner, *The Gospel of John*, 1053.

DAY 36

In a sanctuary, surrounded by brothers and sisters in Christ, we are brave souls, but put us in a university classroom or in an office or at a social gathering, and it's easy to see how denial happens. "Surely you don't believe in this Jesus stuff, do you?" The world expects our agreement and it's easier to go along than to take a stand. We may dodge and deflect, but in the end the right word for it is denial.

What if Peter had not made his proud boast after Jesus had warned the disciples that they were all going to fall away? What if he had said, "Lord, we don't want to fall away! How can we remain strong?" We have a good indication of how Jesus would have answered that question from his response to the exhausted disciples in the garden of Gethsemane. He encouraged them, "Watch and pray so that you will not fall into temptation. The spirit is willing, but the body is weak" (Matt 26:41). If the disciples had returned to the upper room and spent the night in prayer, they would have been more united than isolated. Instead of falling away they might have waited on God. Sadly, it wasn't until after the cross that they returned to the upper room, so to speak, and immersed themselves in prayer.

Upper Room Reflection

Can you see yourself in Peter's reaction?

What is deceptive about the ego challenge?

Where are you most vulnerable to deflection and denial?

How would it have made a difference if the disciples had returned to the upper room and prayed?

DAY 37

The Crowing Rooster

"Very truly I tell you, before the rooster crows, you will disown me three times!" JOHN 13:38

PETER'S DENIAL WAS EMPHATIC. He reinforced it with expletives and oaths (Mark 14:71). A hasty denial might have been said without thinking, and a second chance could have led Peter to reconsider. But instead, his timidity grew, his resolve weakened, and he denied the Lord a second time with more conviction than the first. "I don't know the man!" he announced. By now Peter's rejection had worn a groove in his conscience. Having crossed the line twice, he didn't hesitate to lie and deceive with as much boldness as he was capable of. He called down curses on himself and announced his denial for all to hear. Once, it might have been a moment of weakness quickly taken back. Twice, an unmistakable denial. Three times, an undeniable pattern of denial.

DAY 37

THE ABRASIVE SOUND OF a crowing rooster cutting the predawn quiet reminded Peter of what Jesus said: "Before the rooster crows, you will disown me three times" (John 13:38). Jesus could have simply said that Peter would deny him before dawn. Instead, he tied Peter's awareness to sound rather than to sight. Suddenly, the everyday, early morning sound of the crowing rooster became a soul-penetrating alarm. Peter's memory flashed back to their earlier exchange. He instinctively turned toward Jesus and Luke tells us that "the Lord turned and looked straight at Peter" (Luke 22:61).

Up until this point we are not aware that Jesus and Peter were in visual range. How painful this moment must have been for Jesus. He was being spat upon, punched and slapped, but no blow had the force of Peter's denials (Matt 26:67). The early church found in Psalm 88 a sad description of this painful scene: "You have taken from me my closest friends and have made me repulsive to them. I am confined and cannot escape; my eyes are dim with grief" (Ps 88:8–9). Regardless of the intensity of the abuse he was suffering, he heard the rooster and looked at Peter. Kierkegaard asks, "And how did Christ look at Peter? Was it a repelling look, a look of dismissal? No, it was as a mother sees her child endangered through its own indiscretion; since she cannot approach and snatch the child, she catches him up with a reproachful but also saving look."[1] We are told that Peter "went outside and wept bitterly" (Matt 26:75). The emerging dawn and the sound of the rooster was forever associated in Peter's mind with the blessing of a painful awareness. A necessary blessing on the way to repentance and reconciliation.

Many years ago a friend was arrested for drunk driving and spent a night in jail. To this day the sound of an iron gate clanging shut reminds him of that night when the jail door slammed behind him. Every time a dish falls and breaks, another friend remembers the time she broke a cherished dish belonging to her sister. She swept up the shattered pieces, buried them in the backyard, and never told her sister. Thirty-five years passed before she admitted

---

1. Kierkegaard, *Works of Love*, 166.

to her sister what she had done. Certain sounds trigger the conscience. Did Peter ever forget the deeper meaning of the crowing rooster? Long after forgiveness, the sound of a rooster recalled the pain: the sound of his curse, the look in Jesus' eyes, and the agony of his soul.

But Peter's denial and the crowing rooster are only half the story. The unmistakable sound of the rooster reminded Peter of God's love and mercy. For Peter, the crowing rooster signaled the demise of willful self-rule and ego strength. Pride came to an abrupt end in bitter tears of personal repentance. The night of denial gave way to the morning of deliverance. The sound of the rooster ended the night and heralded the light. It was fitting that some time later, after the resurrection, Jesus restored Peter one morning by the Sea of Galilee. You may recall that Jesus asked Peter three times, "Do you love me?" And Peter answered three times, "Yes, Lord, you know that I love you. . . . Lord, you know all things; you know that I love you" (John 21:15–17).

Later, when the Apostle Peter emphasized the importance of the Word of God, he encouraged believers "to pay attention to it, as to a light shining in a dark place, until the day dawns and the morning star rises in your hearts" (2 Pet 1:19). Peter's reference to the morning star was a reference to his Lord and Savior, Jesus Christ (see Rev 2:28, 22:16), and now when Peter woke in the morning to the sound of a rooster, he was not filled with grief, but with joy. As the psalmist said, "Weeping may remain for a night, but rejoicing comes in the morning" (Ps 30:5). "Satisfy us in the morning with your unfailing love, that we may sing for joy and be glad all our days" (Ps 90:14). No one knew better than Peter the truth of Lamentations 3:23: "Because of the Lord's great love we are not consumed, for his compassions never fail. They are new every morning; great is your faithfulness."

The rooster is a strange biblical image, but it was Jesus who drew it to Peter's attention and subsequently to ours. We were meant to hear the crowing rooster as a reminder to be watchful and vigilant. As Peter said, "Prepare your minds for action; be self-controlled; set your hope fully on the grace to be given you when

Jesus Christ is revealed" (1 Pet 1:13). We were never meant to trust in ourselves or compare ourselves to others. The early morning crowing rooster was an effective daily reminder for Peter and the early church that each new day was to be lived in the presence and power of Jesus Christ. Peter's willful activism was slowly but surely transformed into willed passivity, and among the disciples he became an example of the discipline of surrender. If you don't live within the sound of a crowing rooster you can transfer the soul-triggering significance of the rooster's wake-up call to your alarm clock.

Upper Room Reflection

The crowing rooster provoked pain. How was it a blessing?

Do you agree with Kierkegaard's interpretation of the way Jesus looked at Peter?

If you were Peter would you have been haunted by the sound of a crowing rooster?

Have you experienced repentance as a gift?

DAY 38

Deep Awakening

"I am telling you now before it happens, so that when it does happen you will believe that I am who I am." JOHN 13:19

THE CROSS OF CHRIST overshadows everything said and done in the upper room. We have explored the relationship between the doctrine of the atonement and the praxis of discipleship. We have examined the fault lines running through this text. We have embraced the tension between Jesus' Passion Narrative and our own as we join him on the path of discipleship. Like our Lord we are moving to the cross. From foot-washing to martyrdom, there is a place for us on this continuum of humility and glory. Foot-washing is neither a liturgical rite nor a moralistic act of kindness. God himself on bended knee has given us a way to live that runs counter to the world's understanding of success and significance. Our fallen human quest for recognition and admiration is seen for what it is in the light of Jesus' humility. The honorific culture that pervades the church is critiqued by the humble glory of the God who kneels.

DAY 38

The clash between our fallen human condition and God's redemptive provision strikes at the heart of John 13. The church continues to wrestle with sin-twisted personalities and ambitions along a spectrum that ranges from Peter's ego needs to Judas' self-destructive contempt. Table fellowship in the upper room was the context for exposing and confronting these challenges. Most preaching today takes place in a large room in front of a large audience. The preacher give a sermon and the congregation listens. Little dialogue or interaction exists either before or after the sermon. Instead of wrestling as a group with the implications of what it means to follow Jesus, individuals are left to interpret and apply the sermon for themselves.

English Puritan John Bunyan, author of the classic *The Pilgrim's Progress*, describes in his lesser-known work *Grace Abounding* an encounter with a group of women "sitting at a door in the sun, and talking about the things of God."[1] Bunyan describes their conversation as filled with joy and spiritual depth. They discussed specific Bible passages and applied them personally. Bunyan found their knowledge and sincerity impressive and by observing their true spirituality his own spiritual condition came under review.

Scottish Pastor Alexander Whyte draws an impressive lesson from Bunyan's description. God uses godly, intimate conversation "for the deeper awakening and the deeper undeceiving" of those who follow Christ.[2] Left to ourselves we do not know ourselves. We need a gathering small enough and intimate enough so that true friends can help one another grow in Christ. Preachers alone, no matter how good, cannot produce this soul-searching spiritual formation. But a small group of people who are earnest about their souls will make a difference. "Not a club for questions of theological science, or for questions of Old and New Testament criticism, or even for pulpit and pastoral efficiency," insists Whyte. "But for

---

1. Bunyan, *Grace Abounding*, 18.
2. Whyte, *Bunyan Characters*, 55–57.

questions that are arising within us all every day concerning our own corrupt hearts."[3]

The upper room was the right setting for the deep awakening and deep undeceiving that needed to take place, not only for the original twelve, but for all Christ's disciples. Prayerful meditation on John 13 undermines the misperception that allows for nominal Christianity. There is no room in the upper room for name-only admirers of Jesus. If we cannot find ourselves in this picture of purity of heart and soul-cleansing intimacy with God, then we need to reexamine our relationship with the Lord Jesus. As we have seen, Jesus gently exposed Judas's sham performance and patiently worked with Peter's stubborn character. But the description does not end with two individuals. Instead, it extends to all of us. The God who kneels insists on washing all of the disciples' feet. Figuratively speaking, all who follow Christ belong around this table to be cleansed, redeemed, and discipled.

The whole church fits into the upper room. We all need the scrutiny and intensity of this intimate encounter with Jesus. To receive the God who kneels is to be open to Jesus' soul-defining, life-transforming ministry. The whole church needs his soul-cleansing power and his mission-defining love.

Jesus embodied his teaching ministry in the upper room dramatically. What had been said before was now demonstrated in an act of humility. Jesus contrasted top-down hierarchical leadership with sacrificial service. He disqualified the superior/inferior axis of power and in its place instituted humble service. To be first was to be a slave of all. Jesus linked the praxis of discipleship and the doctrine of the atonement by modeling sacrificial service after his atoning sacrifice.

> "You know that those who are regarded as rulers of the Gentiles lord it over them, and their high officials exercise authority over them. Not so with you. Instead, whoever wants to become great among you must be your servant, and whoever wants to be first must be slave of

3. Ibid., 58.

all. For even the Son of Man did not come to be served, but to serve, and to give his life as a ransom for many" (Mark 10:42–45).

We have seen how Jesus' humility, patience, wisdom, and love grew out of his self-understanding. He knew the hour had come. He knew he was going to leave this world and go to the Father. He knew who were his own and he loved them to the end. He knew the Father had put all things under his power and he knew he had come from God and was returning to God. But in the midst of all of this empowering self-knowledge, there was also the negative knowledge of Judas's betrayal and Peter's denial. Nevertheless, Jesus remained true to his calling and his mission. Life in Christ is like that. Knowing and being known by God does not eliminate conflicts, in fact it only deepens them. If we are going to follow Jesus and obey the will of the Father as he obeyed, and lead the way he led, and love the way he loved, then we are in for a life marked by the cross.

Upper Room Reflection

How does your setting help you embrace the deep truth of John 13?

Why can't nominal Christianity survive in the upper room?

What can we learn from the upper room that inspires effective disciple making?

How have you learned that cross-bearing is not optional?

DAY 39

Our Passion Narrative

"Will you really lay down your life for me?" JOHN 13:38

IN CHRIST WE ENTER into our own passion narrative. We are called to take up our cross daily and follow Jesus. The scandal of the cross, the murder of God, takes place in the midst of political ambiguity and seemingly accidental circumstances. I remember being troubled as a thirteen-year-old by the death of Dr. Paul Carlson, a medical missionary in the Republic of Congo. Carlson was falsely accused by the rebel Simbas of being a major in the American military. His long track record of being a medical doctor and church leader in the Congo was betrayed by false accusations and allegations.

On November 24, 1964, as Belgium paratroopers were landing in Stanleyville, a large group of hostages, including Carlson, were led by their Simba guards out into the middle of the street where they were caught in the cross fire. In the melee some of the hostages were hit, while others ran for cover. A small group ran to the shelter of a house and clambered over the porch wall. One of the hostages leaped over the wall and reached back to grab Carlson. He had his fingers on Paul's sweater when a young Simba rounded

DAY 39

the corner and fired five shots, killing Paul Carlson instantly. A second or two later and he would have been over the wall. As I remember it, his dead body was shown throughout the world on a full page in *Life* magazine.

I questioned God's sovereignty. To my impressionable mind, Dr. Carlson was more a victim of tragic circumstances than an ambassador for Christ who gave his life for the gospel. Since then, I have come to see that the Christian's cross, like Jesus' cross, must be interpreted on two levels. On the one level, confusion and ambiguity surround the meaning of our suffering. From this perspective, Dr. Carlson's death appears meaningless. He was the victim of tragic circumstances that might have been different. Why didn't God give him an extra two seconds to clear the wall?

But seen from another angle, Paul Carlson died like his Lord. The seemingly random circumstances and political upheaval cannot comprehend the deeper meaning of his life and sacrifice. The surface meaning of the accidental moment does not come close to comprehending the orchestrated movement of the sovereign plan of God. Dr. Paul Carlson laid down his life for his Lord.

Jesus appears to be a victim of circumstances—a friend betrays him, popular sentiment turns against him, a ruler concerned only with political expediency hears his case, and his disciples abandon him. But then we grasp a deeper truth. Jesus dies (in accord with Old Testament prophecy) as the lamb who was slain from the foundation of the world (Luke 24:25–27; 1 Pet 1:20; Rev 13:8). There is an inevitability about his death that lies outside historical circumstances and human arrangements. We cannot begin to understand the suffering and death of Jesus apart from God's interpretation of the event. God infuses the cross with meaning from three primary sources: the history of God's revelation to Israel, Jesus' self-disclosure, and the apostolic witness. There is a tremendous redemptive purpose arising out of the muddle of historical circumstances. This glorious purpose is not the product of human imagination and wishful thinking. It is the fulfillment of God's eternal plan of redemption. The real scandal of the cross lies in the fact that God in Christ, the Savior of the world, was crucified.

Four months before Paul Carlson died he preached in Lingala at the Wasolo Regional Church Conference on 1 Peter 2:21–24: "To this you were called, because Christ suffered for you, leaving you an example, that you should follow in his steps.... He himself bore our sins in his body on the tree, so that we might die to sins and live for righteousness; by his wounds you have been healed."

"At this conference," Carlson began, "we are going to think about following Jesus. It is not hard to follow Jesus when all goes well, but sometimes it is difficult to follow Him when the road is difficult."[1] After he described the state of persecution for Christ's sake in various regions in the Congo, he said, "We do not know what will happen in 1964, until we meet together again. We do not know if we will suffer or die during this year because we are Christians. But it does not matter! Our job is to follow Jesus."

From the New Testament, Carlson described the persecution experienced by the early church. "How does all of this apply to us at Wasolo?" Paul asked. "Jesus is asking us if we are willing to suffer for Him. This is of the greatest importance to all of us Christians here today." Then Paul introduced the sacrament of holy communion. He said,

> We are going to gather together at the Lord's Table. Before taking part, I think each person should ask themselves if they are willing to suffer for Jesus Christ if need be—and if he or she is willing even to die if necessary—during this coming year. Taking part in Communion means union with Jesus. Union with Jesus sometimes means joy—but union with Jesus sometimes means suffering. My friends, if today you are not willing to suffer for Jesus, do not partake of the elements. If you do take the cup and bread here today, be certain that you are willing to give your life for Jesus during 1964 or 1965 if it is necessary.

---

1. This and the following quotes from Carlson are from Carlson, *Monganga Paul*, 127–30.

DAY 39

To follow Jesus means to be willing to suffer for Him. Will you follow Jesus this year?

Within two months many of the Congolese believers who heard Carlson's sermon that day and participated in holy Communion were dead. Severe persecution fell heavy on the church. Along with Paul Carlson, these martyrs leave a testimony that inspires and challenges our faithfulness for Christ and his kingdom. Jesus says, "Follow me," and the trajectory of obedience is no mystery.

Upper Room Reflection

We live and die by faith. How does that truth impact our interpretation of Paul Carlson's death?

Do you agree that all Christians live out a passion narrative?

When did you first realize that your life was marked by the cross of Jesus Christ?

What does it mean to you to lay down your life for Christ?

DAY 40

The Third Rejection

"My God, my God, why have you forsaken me?"
MATTHEW 27:46

THERE WAS A THIRD rejection, born not of hate or fear, but of love. This rejection was there from the beginning and informed everything Jesus said and did in the upper room. It was this divine abandonment that preoccupied the mind of Jesus from start to finish. The experience of being Godforsaken was far more painful to Jesus than either Peter's denial or Judas's betrayal. And it was this rejection that ended not in suicide or in repentance, but in salvation. The Father's providential abandonment of the Son is the great theological truth that looms large on Maundy Thursday. Judas's betrayal was based on treachery. Peter's denial was based on timidity. But the Father's relationship was based on trust. The agonizing line from Psalm 22, "My God, my God, why have you forsaken me?" is not quoted in our text, but it lies behind everything said and done in John 13. In a matter of hours Jesus will cry out this lament from the cross and the Apostle John, who sat next to Jesus at the table, will hear it from the foot of the cross (John 19:26).

DAY 40

Jesus exposed Judas's perfidy, confronted Peter's pride, and agonized over the Father's purpose. Any one of these concerns would have been hard enough to endure, but to add up all three only compounds the tremendous burden Jesus was under. We are told how Jesus felt even before he got to the upper room. "Now my heart is troubled, and what shall I say? 'Father, save me from this hour?' No, it was for this very reason I came to this hour. Father, glorify your name!" (John 12:27). It is the Father's rejection for the sake of our salvation that truly accounts for Jesus' deep distress. "My soul is overwhelmed with sorrow to the point of death," Jesus explained to his disciples in Gethsemane. "Abba, Father," Jesus cried, "everything is possible for you. Take this cup from me. Yet not what I will, but what you will" (Matt 26:39). These thoughts were not far removed from Jesus in the upper room when he shed his outer clothing and wrapped a towel around his waist.

Jesus is both one with God and Godforsaken. This is the tension that runs through John 13. He is one with the Father, but forsaken by the Father. For Jesus to be abandoned by the Father, due to our sin and for the sake of our salvation, is the ultimate rejection, and Jesus experienced this all for us. Between foot-washing humility and the humility of being Godforsaken, Jesus was humbled absolutely. There was no other way that Jesus could be humbled. His humility covers the entire range, from mundane menial service to the ultimate divine abandonment. As shocking as Judas's betrayal was it cannot compare to the reality of being Godforsaken: "My God, my God, why have you forsaken me? Why are you so far from saving me, so far from the words of my groaning?" (Psalm 22:1). As disappointing as Peter's denial was it cannot compare to being "stricken by God, smitten by him, and afflicted" (Isa 53:4).

> He was pierced for our transgressions, he was crushed for our iniquities; the punishment that brought us peace was upon him, and by his wounds we are healed. We all, like sheep, have gone astray, each of us has turned to his own way; and the Lord has laid on him the iniquity of us all (Isa 53:5–6).

Judas's betrayal was a cruel sin against humanity. Peter's denial was a sin typical of humanity. But the Father's rejection was *for* the sin of humanity—your sin and mine. Judas's betrayal is shocking; it angers us. Peter's denial is unsettling; it unnerves us. But the Father's rejection humbles us, like nothing else imaginable, and fills us with love for Jesus, who took it all, paid it all, and gave his all, that we might be reconciled to God through him. Because of our Lord and Savior Jesus Christ we live in restored fellowship and redeemed communion with our heavenly Father. Because of him we find ourselves along this redemptive continuum walking the path that Jesus walked. As his followers, we participate in the foot-washing and cross-bearing. The God who kneels empowers us to get down on our knees to wash the feet of others.

Upper Room Reflection

If Jesus was aware of these troubling rejections, why was his upper room teaching so positive and powerful?

Which rejection was the most difficult for Jesus to experience?

If we are never abandoned by the Father, the way Jesus was, why do we resist the will of God?

How can the will of God, even when it means pain and suffering, be motivated out of the Father's deep love for us?

Bibliography

Augustine. "Homilies on The Gospel of John." In *Nicene and Post-Nicene Fathers*, first series, vol. 7, tract 56. Edited by Philip Schaff. Peabody, MA: Hendrickson, 1995.
Beasley-Murray, George R. *John*. Word Biblical Commentary. Waco, TX: Word, 1987.
Bell, Rob. *Love Wins*. New York: Harper One, 2011.
Bonhoeffer, Dietrich. *The Cost of Discipleship*. New York: MacMillan, 1963.
———. *Life Together*. New York: Harper, 1954.
Brand, Paul, and Philip Yancey. "Blood: The Miracle of Cleansing," *Christianity Today*, February 18 and March 4, 1983, 12–15, 38–42.
Bruner, Frederick Dale. *The Gospel of John*. Grand Rapids: Eerdmans, 2012.
Bunyan, John. *Grace Abounding for the Chief of Sinners*. Charleston, SC: BiblioBazaar, 2010.
Carlson, Lois. *Monganga Paul*. New York: Harper & Row, 1966.
Chambers, Oswald. *So Send I You*. London: Marshall, Morgan & Scott, 1964.
Chesterton, G. K. *Orthodoxy*. New York: Image, 1959.
Chrysostom, John. "Homilies on St. John." In *Nicene and Post-Nicene Fathers*, first series, vol. 14. Edited by Philip Schaff. Peabody, MA: Hendrickson, 1995.
———. "To Prove That No One Can Harm the Man Who Does Not Injure Himself." In *Nicene and Post-Nicene Fathers*, first series, vol. 9. Edited by Philip Schaff. Peabody, MA: Hendrickson, 1995.
Defoe, Daniel. *Robinson Crusoe*. Bowser, BC: Aerie, 1989.
Dickinson, Emily. *The Complete Poems of Emily Dickinson*. Edited by Thomas H. Johnson. New York: Little, Brown and Company, 1960.
Edwards, Jonathan. *Charity and Its Fruits*. Carlisle, PA: Banner of Truth, 2005.
Gill, David W. *Peter the Rock: Extraordinary Insights from an Ordinary Man*. Downers Grove, IL: InterVarsity, 1986.
Hawthorne, Gerald F. *Philippians*. Word Biblical Commentary. Waco, TX: Word, 1983.
Jones, Laurie Beth. *Jesus, CEO: Using Ancient Wisdom For Visionary Leadership*. New York: Hyperion, 1995.
Kierkegaard, Søren. *Works of Love*. New York: Harper & Row, 1962.

Luther, Martin. "Sermon for the Thursday Before Easter: Jesus Washes the Feet of His Disciples." In *Sermons on the Gospels for the Sundays and Principal Festivals of the Church Year,* vol. 2, 2nd ed., edited by Matthias Loy, 29-41. Columbus, OH: J. A. Schulze, 1884.

Newbigin, Lesslie. *The Light Has Come: An Exposition of the Fourth Gospel.* Grand Rapids: Eerdmans, 1982.

Niebuhr, H. Richard. *Christ and Culture.* New York: Harper, 1951.

Ortberg, John. "Dallas Willard: A Man for Another Time-Zone." *Christianity Today,* May 8, 2013. http://www.christianitytoday.com/ct/2013/may-web-only/man-from-another-time-zone.html.

Palmer, Parker J. *The Courage to Teach: Exploring the Inner Landscape of a Teacher's Life.* San Francisco: Jossey-Bass, 1998.

Peterson, Eugene H. *Christ Plays in Ten Thousand Places: A Conversation in Spiritual Theology.* Grand Rapids: Eerdmans, 2005.

Rodin, R. Scott. "Notes from the Field: Becoming a Leader of No Reputation." *Journal of Religious Leadership,* vol. 1, no. 2 (Fall 2002) 105–19.

Sittser, Gerald L. *A Grace Disguised: How the Soul Grows Through Loss.* Grand Rapids: Zondervan, 1996.

Tapper, Jake. *The Outpost: An Untold Story of American Valor.* New York: Little, Brown and Company, 2012.

Thielicke, Helmut. *Encounter with Spurgeon.* Philadelphia: Fortress, 1963.

Thomas à Kempis. *The Imitation of Christ.* Milwaukee: Catholic Way, 2013.

Webster, Jeremiah. "Modern Mandrake: Reviving the Poetry of T. S. Eliot." In *Paradise in The Waste Land by T. S. Eliot,* 1–19. Milwaukee: Wiseblood, 2013.

Whyte, Alexander. *Bunyan Characters.* Grand Rapids: Baker, 1981.

Willimon, William. "Interview with William Willimon: A New Evaluative Question: 'Would Jesus Have to Be Crucified to Make This Sermon Work?" *Modern Reformation,* November/December 2000, 41–46.

www.ingramcontent.com/pod-product-compliance
Lightning Source LLC
Chambersburg PA
CBHW022123160426
43197CB00009B/1136